THE UNIVERSITY OF NORTH CAROLINA
SOCIAL STUDY SERIES

AMONG THE DANES

THE UNIVERSITY OF NORTH CAROLINA
SOCIAL STUDY SERIES

ODUM AND JOHNSON: *The Negro and His Songs*	$3.00
PUCKETT: *Folk Beliefs of the Southern Negro*	5.00
ODUM AND JOHNSON: *Negro Workaday Songs*	3.00
ODUM AND OTHERS: *Southern Pioneers*	2.00
POUND: *Law and Morals*	2.00
GIDDINGS: *The Scientific Study of Human Society*	2.00
ODUM AND WILLARD: *Systems of Public Welfare*	2.00
BRANSON: *Farm Life Abroad*	2.00
ROSS: *Roads to Social Peace*	1.50
WILLEY: *The Country Newspaper*	1.50
JORDAN: *Children's Interests in Reading*	1.50
ODUM: *Public Welfare and Social Work*	1.50
NORTH: *Social Differentiation*	2.50
KNIGHT: *Among the Danes*	2.00

A View of Askov Folk High School

AMONG THE DANES

By EDGAR WALLACE KNIGHT
Professor of Education
University of North Carolina

CHAPEL HILL
THE UNIVERSITY OF NORTH CAROLINA PRESS
LONDON: HUMPHREY MILFORD
OXFORD UNIVERSITY PRESS
1927

COPYRIGHT, 1927, BY
THE UNIVERSITY OF NORTH CAROLINA PRESS

PRESSES OF
EDWARDS & BROUGHTON COMPANY
RALEIGH

PREFACE

During the school year 1925-1926 opportunity was offered me, through a leave of absence granted on the Kenan Foundation of the University of North Carolina and by appointment as Research Fellow of the Social Science Research Council, to visit and study certain types of schools and education in Scandinavia. Shortly after beginning the study it seemed wise to limit the scope of the work, and as a result most of the period was given to an investigation of education in Denmark. Notes dealing with various educational and cultural agencies in that country were published by seven North Carolina dailies in their Sunday editions during my absence and for a short time after my return to the United States. Those articles, which were intended for popular reading, have now been revised and appear in the following pages. In the main the notes deal with those economic, social, and educational efforts in Denmark which have transformed that little country and made it one of the best educated and most intelligent countries in Europe.

The reasons for selecting Denmark as a place of study are given in the initial chapter. Until the middle of the last century that country was affected primarily by economic, social, and political movements and influences from other countries. About 1850, however, internal conditions served to arouse and free certain forces which led to a remarkable awakening. The national spirit of the Danes began to assert itself and to take definite form. Principles of progress somewhat peculiar to the Danish people began to be established and national ideals soon became the possession of all. Denmark began in years of struggle and sacrifice to create a civilization worthy of her hopes and aspirations,—years of discouragement not altogether unlike that experienced by the people in the southern part of the United States during that long period of slow and painful recovery from the devastating results of war and reconstruction after 1865. Historically there are some rather close parallels between Denmark and the Southern States.

Today a wholesome civilization has become so widespread among the Danes as to be in large part the heritage of the humblest citizen. It is a civilization which reflects the spirit of the people themselves. It has been built by education, that master builder in Denmark, which has constructed an attractive and profitable rural life. A visitor viewing the conditions there is convinced that what schools have done for this rural country, schools can do also for the rural people of the United States, where richer and more abundant educational resources must be provided if a majestic civilization of wholesomeness, of culture, of beauty, of imagination and thought is to be made active in the life of the people themselves.

Denmark is quietly removed from the vortex of European politics. The country is free from internal disturbances, unambitious to extend her own territorial dominions, perhaps not jealous enough of her national greatness, but calmly and very effectively looking after her own affairs. It is a romantic land with a history of picturesque variety and adventure, a quite creditable literature, a music noteworthy for tunefulness and simplicity, many remarkable antiquities, a most gentle and lovely people, and many other interesting and attractive possessions.

Perhaps Denmark is best known abroad, however, for the remarkable coöperative agencies which began and have developed there, for her exceedingly good system of popular education, for the numerous and excellent agricultural schools, and for the rather remarkable plan for adult education which is furnished through the so-called folk high schools or people's colleges. To see and examine the folk high schools was one of the objects of the visit. A separate and more detailed account of these schools as they appeared to the visitor is to be published shortly.

The present volume contains observations and impressions of a variety of practices which reflect the essentially democratic ideals prevailing in this northern country. In many ways Denmark appears to have made democracy a reality. It is one of the few countries in the world now using fully the machinery and power of the state to promote the economic well-being of the people and to advance their educational and cultural life as well. The Danes have developed great confidence in the function of government; they show less concern than we in this country for its machinery. They have made government serve the people, who they believe constitute the government, and for whose welfare government is established and should be maintained.

Moreover, the Danes appear very courageous in facing real social and political problems. Good schools have purified their politics, dignified their ways of government, and enlightened the people. Through education and coöperation the Danes have reduced social injustice and increased the well-being of all the people. They have applied taxation, which is quite high in Denmark, as investment in common prosperity, preferring the pressure of taxation, however heavy, to any load of ignorance and the dangers which walk in its steps, however light. And yet the Danish government is not conducted as a charity organization.

There are numerous lessons which the Danes may teach the rural sections of the United States, which contain some of the most persistent and stubborn problems in American life at this moment. In the Danish system of education are lessons for the rural communities which abound in the United States, especially in the southern part of this country. Now for more than a hundred years Denmark has ordered that education shall be the possession of all the people, rural and urban alike.

The result of this provision is that there is discernible almost everywhere in Denmark a strong and natural antipathy or aversion toward ignorance. There is also evident almost everywhere in that country an attitude of deep respect for sound learning. The Danes seem ashamed of ignorance and stupidity and seize upon every opportunity to increase their knowledge. Popular education in variety and abundance has made the rural people of Denmark perhaps the most intelligent rural people in the world. It has broadened their sympathies and helped to produce a type of mind which is capable of receiving and of profiting by expert knowledge, which the Danes greatly respect and by which they are eager to be guided.

Denmark is not afflicted with complicated educational machinery, numerous minute statutes and regulations, or those other fitful expediencies, which too often wear less the color of settled policy than that of pious aspiration, for which too many American states have often disclosed especial fondness. For these states there are some lessons in the simple plan which the Danes have set up for the education of their children and themselves. A very simple plan it is, but the spirit of education in it is bounteous and liberal, and transcends and rises above machinery. This does not mean the absence of educational standards which are high and creditable. It does mean, however, that the externalities of education have not been allowed to mechanize its spirit. In Denmark the purpose of the school is not allowed to become lost in the details of school administration.

For the rural people of the United States there are important lessons also in Danish agriculture, for which the Danes are perhaps best known. The high place of farming, which is a business with the Danes, has been made by education. Agricultural science has given an almost æsthetic aspect to farming, even in the cultivation of pigs. It has made out of farming an occupation of great dignity and one that is viewed as indispensable in the national economy. The success of Danish agriculture is due also to the coöperative interests and activities which are so widely known abroad, and which education and training in collective action have made possible. Students generally, in Denmark and elsewhere, who are familiar with the recent history and development of this interesting country unite in the belief that the prosperity and contentment of the rural people are due almost entirely to the kind and universality of education provided in that country. It has removed illiteracy, reduced and prevented poverty and delinquency, made farm tenancy a thing of the past, and raised the level of intelligence and culture among the masses of the rural people. These same achievements can be made for the rural people of the United States as they have been made for the people of Denmark,—by the people themselves, who have provided the means of adequate educational opportunity for all. The problem there was one which called for enlightened leadership which is so much needed in the rural sections of the United States. The ways by which it has been solved in Denmark the following notes indicate, at least in part.

EDGAR W. KNIGHT.

THE UNIVERSITY OF NORTH CAROLINA
October, 1926.

CONTENTS

I	A Preliminary View	1
II	Jeppe on the Hill	11
III	The Prophet of the North	22
IV	The Midgard Snake	34
V	Checking the Waste	51
VI	A Folk High School	63
VII	Adult Education	73
VIII	The Enchanter of the North	84
IX	Slesvig and National Minorities	95
X	Education and National Minorities	104
XI	Training Elementary Teachers	115
XII	Training High School Teachers	127
XIII	Winning Higher Degrees	139
XIV	Commencement Exercises	149
XV	Respect for Learning	159
XVI	Education and Agriculture	170
XVII	Taxes	187
XVIII	Marriage and Divorce in Denmark	200
XIX	The Decay of Romance	212
XX	Social Welfare	224

ILLUSTRATIONS

A VIEW OF ASKOV HIGH SCHOOL. . . . .*Frontispiece*
                                              FACING PAGE
BIRTHPLACE OF HANS CHRISTIAN ANDERSEN. 87
A STATE NORMAL SCHOOL. 129
ANOTHER VIEW OF ASKOV HIGH SCHOOL. 183

AMONG THE DANES

CHAPTER I

A Preliminary View

IMMEDIATELY after the announcement at commencement in the spring of 1925 that the trustees of the University of North Carolina had afforded opportunity for a study of education in Denmark, the chief inquiry made of the prospective visitor to that country was:

"Why do you go to Denmark? What have the Danes to show North Carolinians or other Americans in such matters as schools? Would not a study of education in France, particularly in and about Paris, be more inviting and interesting? Besides, is it not very cold in Scandinavia?"

The answer always was that Denmark was chosen because that country was reported to have a highly creditable system of general education, of elementary and secondary schools, very effective plans for training and pensioning teachers, and other very successful educational agencies that the people of the United States, especially of the Southern States, or other rural areas, might find suggestive. Among these agencies are the agricultural schools and especially the folk high schools, which are attended by adults and which have been given credit for many of the remarkable achievements for a better rural civilization in that north country. The folk high schools, which originated in Denmark, have had a wide influence among the Danes, have helped to remake rural life in that country, and have increased the prosperity and contentment of the rural people.

The visitor desired to learn, if possible, the secret of the effectiveness and success of the Danish folk high schools and to see if that secret could be used in certain rural sections of the United States. These schools, which have no admission requirements, no examinations, and give no credits, are said to awaken, to enliven, and to enlighten the people who attend them. Requirements for admission, rigid examinations, and so-called credits which must be measured, weighed, certificated, recorded, card-indexed, and rewarded by diplomas are such constant features of school work in the United States that it seemed worth a trip across the ocean to see schools which have much to do with education and little to do with its machinery and externalities.

To awaken, to enliven, and to enlighten are very worthy and substantial educational objectives; but schools which so influence many people in the rural sections of the United States are very few. Denmark is said to have many schools which do these things for many rural people every year. If they can be built and maintained in rural Denmark, why can they not be set up and directed for the rural people of the American states? One purpose of the visit, therefore, was to gather some first-hand information on the Danish rural schools. And the chief purpose of these notes was to furnish that information as clearly as possible, to interpret these schools in relation to government and to the life of the people and in the light of the conditions out of which they have grown, and to indicate any lessons which Denmark may have for education in rural America.

For many years Denmark has been attracting the attention of students from all over the world.

They have come here in large numbers from the United States in the hope of seeing that remarkable civilization which has been built up during the last half century or so, and of learning its secret. The unique coöperative institutions of Denmark and the social and political conditions out of which they have grown have been written about and discussed by students and observers, by Englishmen, and Frenchmen, and Germans, and Americans, and by the Danes themselves. They have reported on the lively agricultural system, the thrifty coöperative agencies, the effective educational plans, and many other civilizing agencies of the country by which Danish culture has been revived, restored, and increased. These agencies have helped to produce a remarkably substantial, prosperous, and happy rural life in Denmark, which is said to have the broadest and most generous culture of any country in Europe.

The work of education in Denmark as the primary agency of improvement and enlightment will claim most attention in these notes. But a school system can best be understood in the light of its origin and its political, social, economic, and geographical environment. From time to time, therefore, it may appear necessary to lead through some of the history of this remarkable little country to the conditions which now surround education in it. Most of that history is heroic, noble, and inspiring. Brief summary accounts will be made of some of the significant facts of Danish political and social history, something will be said about the Danish people themselves, and the land they live in, and the like. The general school system will be briefly described, the relation between government and education will be noted, and something will be said of the manner by which the schools reflect an ideal of government as an agency for promoting the well-being of all the people.

"Where and what is this very remarkable country you have been writing about?" a friend asked a few days ago. It had not seemed necessary to describe this little Scandinavian land whose description may be found in geographies and in encyclopedias and other books of reference; and but little of its geographic location and size, its history, its present form of government, and the like was included in the notes published in the papers. Now, however, it seems desirable to include a few words on these and other matters, because a knowledge of Northern Europe is probably not very wide among general readers in the United States.

The kingdom of Denmark is quite small in area. It is about one-third the size of New York or of North Carolina, one-fourth the size of Iowa, and about twice the size of Massachusetts. The country is made up of the peninsula of Jutland, which joins the continent of Europe and divides the North Sea from the Baltic, and of the islands of Zealand, Funen, Lolland, Bornholm, Falster, Möen, and numerous other smaller islands, many of which are uninhabited. The country abounds in small lakes and water courses, but as the coast is nowhere very distant none of the latter can attain any respectable size. Of the entire land area, the really productive soil—that is, the soil under cultivation—and the forest areas constitute about ninety-four per cent of the islands and about eighty-three per cent of Jutland. Bogs, heaths and heather hills, drift-sands and dunes, all for the most part unproductive, constitute a not inconsiderable area, although some of this has been restored to fertility in recent years, under the direction of the Danish Heath Society, whose activities are described in chapter six. The heaths and dunes are found in largest number in Jutland and form a continuous line along the west coast of that peninsula to the Scaw. About seventy years ago, however, the planting of some of these areas was completed and the destruction caused by the drifting sands was reduced. More recently cultivation has been started on some of the heaths, and rather large areas have been turned into forests, plantations, and other productive lands. Of the productive portion of the area of Denmark the agricultural part is the most important.

The country forms a part of the Northern European lowland, with an average elevation of less than one hundred feet above the level of the sea. The land is not naturally fertile, comprising mainly moraine clays and moraine sands and peat bogs. Nature has not been very kind to Denmark. Her wide reputation for great agricultural production is not due to rich natural endowments but to the application of the intelligence of the Danes to the often discouraging task of making and maintaining the fertility of the soil. The climate, moreover, is naturally a markedly coastal climate which, while somewhat inhospitable, has a higher average temperature than that of many places on the same parallel of latitude. It is generally cold and damp in winter and cloudy days are numerous. Fogs are not uncommon and Copenhagen, somewhat favorably located, cannot boast of many days of sunshine. Cattle must be stall-fed eight or nine months out of the twelve. In spite of all these natural handicaps, however, the Danes have converted a poorly ordered agricultural system into one of the best in the world,—through education and intelligence.

The population of Denmark is very homogeneous. Immigration of foreign elements has been so slight that only here and there has it left any traces upon the people. The Danes are of the Gotho-Germanic race which has inhabited the country since prehistoric times. The Danish language is spoken almost everywhere although there are dialects and "accents" in Jutland which differ from the language used in Zealand and especially in Copenhagen. Denmark is one of the fairly well populated countries of Europe, having now close to three and one-half million people.

A little more than fifty per cent of the people live in the capital and its neighboring communities of Frederiksberg and Gentofte and in the eighty-five provincial towns and some seventy-five or more suburban districts and other urban localities. The capital which in reality includes the three towns built close together (Copenhagen, Frederiksberg and Gentofte) is the largest city in Denmark and contains almost a fourth of the total Danish population. Aarhus is the next largest town with about seventy-five thousand people. Odense, in Funen, has around fifty thousand; Horsens and Randers, in East Jutland, have each about twenty-eight thousand inhabitants; Esbjerg, in West Jutland, has about twenty-three thousand people; and Aalborg, in North Jutland, has about forty-three thousand people. The other provincial towns of Denmark are generally quite small. Fifty years ago the urban population comprised about one-fourth of the people of the entire kingdom, but now, largely as a result of the development of industries and commerce and the increasing tendency to specialization, it comprises about one-half the population. Moreover, the extensive use of machinery in Denmark has made it possible for agriculture to be carried on with fewer workers than formerly. The larger number of the people are engaged in agriculture, forestry, fisheries, handicraft, and industry.

Denmark, which is a constitutional monarchy, is known as one of the most democratic countries in the world. Its democracy is broad and practical. From about the middle of the seventeenth century to the middle of the nineteenth century the Danes had lived under a system of absolute monarchy and the autocratic principle operated fully. In 1849, however, King Frederik the Seventh permitted a free constitution without having been urged by revolution to do so and this constitution was established upon rather far reaching democratic principles. This rather liberal constitution was amended, however, in 1866, when for a time the more wealthy and influential people regained some power in the Upper House of Parliament, known as the *Landsting*, while the Lower House, known as the *Folketing*, remained practically unchanged.

A few years later the more democratic element of the population, whose stronghold was in the agricultural classes, gained considerable strength in the *Folketing* and a very keen constitutional conflict arose. The struggle was carried on with some bitterness though without actual disturbances, and the conservative strength more and more lost ground among the people; and more and more were democratic ideas spread abroad among them, resulting in considerable influence on the social and economic development of the country. About 1901 the struggle ended with the appointment of a cabinet which was in sympathy with the majority in the Lower House; and since that time this parliamentary principle has been the generally acknowledged basis of the constitutional system of Denmark. Many practical reforms were worked during the early years of the present century, but the question of further constitutional improvement came up again during the World War, when the Danish people succeeded in agreeing upon a new constitutional act in June, 1915. For the most part this revised constitution marked a return to the constitution of 1849, but with the introduction of certain modern ideas which meantime had been generally acknowledged.

Under the Danish constitution legislative authority now rests jointly with the Crown and with Parliament. The executive power is vested in the Crown, the administration of justice is exercised by the courts, the king exercises authority through the cabinet which he appoints and which is responsibile for the government of the country. The members of the cabinet may be impeached by the king or the *Folketing* in matters touching the discharge of their official duties. The king cannot, without the sanction of parliament, declare war or conclude peace, nor can he enter into or sever alliances or commercial treaties, cede any part of the country, or enter into any obligation which alters its constitutional status. All men and women who are of Danish nationality and twenty-five years of age and permanently residing in Denmark have the right of the franchise, unless sentence has been passed upon them by the courts for a dishonorable offense, or unless they have been in receipt of poor relief, or are undischarged bankrupts, or are declared incapable of managing their affairs. The proportional system of representation is in general use in state and local elections. The country is divided into twenty-two counties and the central government participates in local government through the administration of a governor in each county. Local government in the provincial towns and the rural communities generally, however, is in the hands of local officials.

The Evangelical Lutheran Church is the established religion of Denmark, and until near the middle of the last century all Danish subjects were obliged to belong to this church. Under the constitution of 1849, however, religious liberty was introduced. Compulsory baptism was expressly abolished and civil forms of marriage and burial were allowed. Under the present constitution the Lutheran Church is the established church to which the king must belong, and which must be supported by the State. Legislation regarding the church is enacted in the same manner as all other laws of the kingdom, but church laws since the middle of the last century have been marked by great respect for religious liberty.

No person is obliged to belong to the church or to accept the ministrations of the parish to which he belongs. Free congregations may be formed to choose and support their own ministers, even without being regarded as having left the Established Church, whose church buildings such congregations have a right to use. Moreover, free congregations may be formed outside the Established Church with full and complete liberty as to belief and manner of worship. In spite of these liberal provisions, however, only about 70,000 people in Denmark are not members of the Established Church. The other denominations most strongly represented are the Catholics, Jews, Reformists, Methodists, Baptists, and Irvingites.

About the time the states which formed the Southern Confederacy of the United States were devastated and almost destroyed, Denmark found herself in distress, her political, social, and economic structure about to totter and the people greatly discouraged. The country was, quite like the Southern States, discredited. The way out of that plight the Danes sought in education, a rather remarkable school system which furnishes a broad culture and a thorough technical preparation to all the people living in the rural sections of Denmark. Since 1864 she has restored herself, has developed an effective system of general education and of adult and agricultural education, perfected an agricultural system that is unexcelled anywhere, created coöperative agencies which are the marvel of Europe and America, removed illiteracy among the people, converted tenants into owners of homes, organized the farmers and enabled them to protect their interests, and brought to the masses of the Danish people a high level of intelligence and culture and material prosperity. Education has transformed rural Denmark. The right kind of education properly directed can transform any rural community in the United States. Some of the ways by which the Danes have done these things for themselves will be indicated in the notes to follow.

CHAPTER II

JEPPE ON THE HILL

MORE than seven hundred years ago there came a brilliant embassy from far away Denmark to the court of King Ottocar of Bohemia to ask the hand of his daughter, Dagmar, for King Valdemar, the ruler of the Danes. In their ancient tongue Dagmar meant daybreak, and it seemed that a new and beautiful day dawned upon Denmark with the arrival of Dagmar; she "came without burden, she came with peace, she came the good peasant to cheer." In those days it was the custom and the privilege of the bride to ask a gift of her husband on the morning after the wedding and he must grant it without question or quibble. The story is told in Denmark that the boon or favor which Dagmar craved "right early in the morning, long before it was day," was that the peasant might be relieved of the burdensome "plow tax," and that those peasants who, for resisting it, had been put in prison might be set free. The request was granted; and seven centuries have not dimmed in Denmark the memory of the good queen whose interest was in the peasant and the poor. The Danes yet sing her praises.

The granting of the request of Queen Dagmar by King Valdemar may be taken as the significant beginning of an important movement in Denmark. The rise of the rural underclass, which had almost no culture or technical skill, from sullen dependence upon large landed proprietors, estate owners, and government officials to a class which now constitutes the leadership of the country, is one of the romantic and picturesque chapters in Danish history. This remarkable change in the condition of the peasants is closely related to the reforms in education and especially to the influence of the folk high schools or people's colleges and the agricultural schools, which must be credited in large part with the transformation.

Ludvig Holberg, one of the greatest comedy writers of all time, often called the Danish Molière, wrote in the early part of the eighteenth century one of his most significant pieces, called *Jeppe paa Bjerget* (Jeppe on the Hill).[1] The comedy portrays the conversion of a coarse and drunken peasant into a gentleman of power. Jeppe, the peasant, while drunk, is taken to a manor and is made to believe that he is the baron. For several days he is allowed to use the powers becoming a baron but he does so in a very crude and foolish manner. Soon he becomes drunk again and is returned to the squalid conditions out of which he had temporarily been taken. The play ends with the real baron declaiming the philosophy that to elevate those of low rank above their proper place is as perilous an experiment in sociology and government as to destroy by rash revolution the great and powerful who have become so by "deeds of just renown." If the baseborn is permitted untutored sway, it is pointed out, the symbol of government becomes a scourge. The moral thus declaimed is a warning against the dictates of boors.

---

[1] The rise of the Danish peasantry is described in the *Folk High Schools of Denmark and the Development of a Farming Community*, by Holger Begtrup, Hans Lund, and Peter Manniche, Oxford University Press, 1926. Through the courtesy of Mr. Manniche, the book was examined in manuscript and furnished the suggestion of the title for this chapter and a part of the material used in it.

This comedy was performed in the Royal Theatre in Copenhagen shortly after the farmer class in Denmark, in the early part of the present century, had come into political power and had formed a liberal ministry. For the first time in all Danish history this class had secured positions in the cabinet and had begun to take charge of political affairs. When on this occasion the moral to the comedy was declaimed there was great applause from the audience which was made up in large part of conservatives who thus announced to the new "peasant" ministry that they had the great writer in their support as the opponent of the rule of peasant power.

A liberal Danish newspaper, however, pointed out editorially about that time that the moral of the play did not longer apply, because conditions had greatly changed. Very remarkable changes had taken place in the baron as well as in the peasant since the play was written. The baron had failed to retain all or very much of his culture and refinement and interests; he had become stupid, perhaps somewhat degenerate, and had failed at government. The peasant was not now the drunkard he once was. He had been freed from serfdom, had stopped his carousals, had begun to improve himself, had united with others to cultivate his fields better and to sell his products to greater advantage than ever before, had turned his attention to the educational improvement of his children, and was also taking an active interest in political matters. So great was the peasant's improvement that his friends wanted to send him over to Copenhagen as a member of Parliament. So Jeppe stepped up to the ministers who had become careless in their duties and said in substance: "Sorry, barons, but you must be tired. We have come to relieve you for a period. We are sorry that we are a trifle late in arriving."

This is practically what has happened in Denmark. It is a fair picture of Danish development in the last century. Less than one hundred years ago the farmers of Denmark were in a deplorable state. Today they are the leaders of Danish life. Education has produced the change. Then they were surrounded by abject conditions, cowed, dazed, not different from the underclasses of other European countries. Some agricultural improvements had been made by others in behalf of the peasants, but they themselves gave no aid and did not understand the significance of such reforms. The great committee for agricultural reorganization had on it not a single representative of the class for whom the reforms were principally designed. The early agricultural reforms therefore, were made for but not by the farmer classes. And when freedom was offered to them they were not qualified to benefit by the possibilities which the reforms held. Interest in agricultural theories was then found only among the big farmers. Agricultural journals were edited by manufacturers and merchants; the chief contributions were by ministers and tradesmen and large landed proprietors and industrial people, who also formed and promoted the first agricultural societies. The most practical guides on agriculture before the middle of the last century were prepared not by farmers but by clergymen. All of these efforts to improve the condition of the peasant or small farming and tenant class were more or less humanitarian and philanthropic in character.

A tendency towards independence began to appear in the early forties, in a class consciousness by which the peasants sought to secure a change from tenants to freeholders. The constitution of 1849 also helped; moreover, the educational conditions of the people had slightly improved under the school plan set up in 1814 and strengthened later; economic conditions had become a bit better and there was thus released some of the potential power of the poorer classes which hitherto had been used entirely in gaining a bare existence—a condition not unknown in the Southern States for several decades following the Civil War. In 1840 there were a score of agricultural societies, but they were all led by large estate owners. By 1864 another score had been formed, and by 1900 more than one hundred such organizations were in operation. But by this time they had become the farmers' own organizations. Meantime, a movement had been gaining strength for savings banks for the support and in the interest of agriculture. By the middle of the nineteenth century about forty had been organized; by 1864 there were nearly twice that number, and by the end of the century there were fully five hundred such banks in Denmark. These came almost completely under the control of the peasants and farmers who were by this time giving evidence of growing pride and progress.

Denmark had an agricultural crisis in the seventies. European markets were flooded with products from America and the Argentine, and Danish farmers were greatly injured. But the crisis proved a blessing, because they began to produce corn for home consumption and for making butter and bacon. Under the force of these conditions dairying and the breeding of cattle extended —the Danes even by this time had learned the importance of adjusting themselves to the changed conditions. They were able to adopt new methods which the changes required. Through the influence of education, especially that given in the folk high schools, they were then as now able to take in and use new ideas. But for this capacity to change their methods to meet changed conditions the Danes might have stubbornly held on to conservative ideas and invited disaster in the crisis which they then faced.

It was largely the folk high schools which had produced this capacity in the Danes and had demonstrated to the skeptics that their work had not developed ineffectual dreamers. They had helped to raise the standard of adult education and had really shown how quickly an energetic and ambitious person between 18 and 25 years of age could be prepared for and directed in fuller living among and for his fellows. For it was the pupils from these schools who had led the way in most of the improvement and had pointed out the need also for technical agricultural education. These pupils also helped to organize and later got control of the coöperative agencies which promoted agriculture among the people. It was through their influence that the agricultural colleges were established, and these very effective schools now number about twenty-one.

The agricultural schools grew up to meet the need for technical instruction in agriculture and are one of the concrete results of the folk high schools, with which they are closely affiliated. They are organized very much like the folk high schools and some of them follow similar methods of instruction, which is not technical only but contains general high school work as well. Especially is this true of the schools for gardeners and the small holders. A period at the folk high school is usually regarded as good preparation for the agricultural schools and many men and women have been students in both.

The influence of the agricultural schools is already generally well known. An encyclopedia of biographies of distinguished Danes in various activities shows that considerably more than one hundred farmers, leading men in Danish agriculture, have earned distinction, and most of these have been students in the folk high schools and the agricultural schools. These men have been engaged in practical work, in coöperation, in education, and in politics. Fully four-fifths of the rural leaders of Denmark have attended these schools. Kraks' *Blue Book*, the Danish *Who's Who*, showing the biographies of the living Danes who have become distinguished in the social life of Denmark, contains the names of about 130 men who have lived in agricultural circles and most of them are former folk high school pupils. These cold statistics are supported by the warmer evidence of a rather universal popular judgment in Denmark that these schools have inspired and given support to most of the movements which have had as their aim the advancement of rural life. Dr. L. Moltesen, the inspector of the folk high schools and the agricultural schools, himself now a member of Parliament, writes in a letter on the subject that thirty-five per cent of the present members of Parliament and four of the twelve ministers are former students of these excellent educational institutions.

The change from a helpless peasant to a reliable, substantial, and socially and politically powerful farmer is one of the stories of Danish life which must be viewed if the full meaning of the folk high school movement is to be gained. Other influences have worked at the same time to produce this remarkable change but it is to the folk high school movement that large credit must be given for the economic recuperation and the educational and general cultural advance of the rural population of Denmark in recent years. It would be extravagant to say that all reform movements there had their inspiration in and received all practical support from the folk high schools. But much, if indeed not most, of the advanced agricultural and social legislation which seems so distinctive in Denmark can be traced directly or indirectly to such influences.

The leaders in these movements for rural regeneration and enlightenment in Denmark gained in these schools the preparation for the difficult tasks which they have performed so well. They have exhibited enlarged outlook, strengthened character, ambition for knowledge, the feeling for fellowship, and a desire to have some part in promoting the commonwealth. They are marked by devotion to their country and pride in her achievements. These possessions were gained in large part from the folk high schools, or the people's colleges which they now prefer to be called. They have taught the nobility and the greatness of the simple, the common, and useful tasks,—the poetry of active and practical human activities in rural communities. The teaching of history has also played a large part in this. History, it may be recalled, was one of the subjects which Grundtvig insisted on as fundamental in the work of the folk high schools; and among the most conspicuous of the instructors observed in the many institutions visited were those lively teachers of history, whose work there strengthens one's faith in the power of historical information for changing and improving and enlivening men and women. This power is evident in rural Denmark where this lofty view of agriculture has been presented to so many of the people who through coöperative agencies daily glorify and adorn the tasks of the workaday farming world. In Denmark farming is not viewed as drudgery,—and this is yet another lesson which the rural people of the United States could learn if they could have such agricultural instruction as may be found in Denmark.

The Jeppe in Holberg's comedy represents the results of a debasing social and economic system. In him, however, may be seen glimpses of native shrewdness and vigor of will that have made the farmer class such a vital part of Denmark today. But there is one important difference between the outcome of the comedy and what has actually happened to the peasant in real life during the last hundred years. Jeppe, as delineated by Holberg, was a wretch cowed into abject submission to everything and everybody, including his wife who beat him, the bailiff who worked him as a beast of burden, and even the deacon who shamelessly made of him a cuckold. When he awakened to find himself in the baron's gorgeous bed and attended by many obsequious servants, power meant to him the opportunity to be despotic and arbitrary. It seems natural also, as George Brandes says, "for the man who has worked like a horse to take his pleasures like a dog." It is also natural that he should select his victims from the class of men who had so long abused him.

The Jeppe in real life, however, has used his power for quite different purposes. And now those in Denmark who recall the romantic story of the change in the rural people from a benighted and underprivileged class to an enlightened and privileged one say that if Holberg should return to his beloved Scandinavia he would rewrite his comedy and present a different picture. Peasant Jeppe would now be revealed, as a result of education and coöperation, as superior to the baron in the politics and economics of government. He removed landlordism, he made the state lend him money to buy farms, transport him and his produce, provide him and his family with sick benefits and pensions in old age, and in other ways he has had the state enable him and his fellows to become landowners, members of Parliament, cabinet ministers, and advisors to the crown. The baron would doubtless be portrayed as ineffective and perhaps even stupid and useless in such work.

Jeppe, in the revised comedy, would declaim the moral. He would probably indicate the great risk taken by those people who continue to select their rulers and lawmakers because of their estate, their wealth, and their hereditary nobility. He would urge respect for and recognition of the aristocracy of intellect and character, self-reliance and initiative. Perhaps he should also urge the people not to become too dependent upon the state whose benevolence and benefactions if abused must send them back to the sorry place from which Jeppe in drunken stupor was removed.

Few countries have done so much or are doing so much now as Denmark is doing for the people. In some respects it may seem too much, but something more is said on that point in another chapter. If the people remain self-reliant and thrifty the future of rural Denmark will be bright. If they become blindly dependent upon the State, however, as the underclasses were once dependent upon the landed proprietors, the estate owners, and the government officials, their last serfdom will be worse than the first, and the economic and spiritual structure of little Denmark will collapse. Such an outcome is not likely so long as the Danes continue to educate and train themselves as properly as they now seem to do.

CHAPTER III

THE PROPHET OF THE NORTH

THE foremost works of the newer pedagogical literature are *The Origin of Species* and *The Descent of Man*. Although Charles Darwin did not write a word about education save a few remarks on his own experiences from his school days, his works about evolution have founded the reform movements which are running through the schools today. The theory of evolution, which was practically introduced into science by the works of Charles Darwin, has been the motive which gave rise to the energetic study of the physical and mental evolution of the child, a study which rational pedagogy in the future will make the basis of its researches."

These were the words of Wilhelm Rasmussen, author of a score of books,—many of which have been translated into French, German, English, and Russian,—teacher, scientist, member of the Danish Parliament, and just now principal of the Danish High School for Teachers, perhaps the most responsible and highly honored teaching position in all Denmark. He had invited a North Carolina visitor to his home on a cold day in January, and one of the many questions he answered was:

"What is your explanation of Denmark's high educational position? Who were most influential in blazing the way for the progress of Denmark, for building the hospitable attitude of the Danes toward science, the enlightened and yet democratic manner of living, and the very widespread and impressive interest which you have in childlife here?"

The influence of two men, Dr. Rasmussen thought, was in large part responsible for the development of Denmark. One of these men was Charles Darwin. And he pointed out that the great educators before Darwin really did not study the child systematically. He pointed to Rousseau, Pestalozzi, Froebel, and to others who wrote and worked mainly on the basis of their personal experiences. Their genius and sympathy made them natural observers and intuitive interpreters of children. But a systematic study and a rational interpretation of childhood was not put to use, he thought, until the first editions of *The Origin of Species* and *The Descent of Man* had appeared and the discussion of evolution had begun in earnest. In recent years, he pointed out, a steady stream of books about the mental evolution of the child had poured forth from the press. And he went on to say that the art of education (he thinks education is an art rather than a science) may as well as any other art be developed further when based upon the scientific approach. Psychology, he said, makes one a more careful observer of children and enables one to understand more clearly the causes of their behavior.

"The high goal of education is to give to each child the opportunity for carrying on its personal development to the highest possible level, according to its natural equipment. Education is a process of adapting children to conditions about them. But today it is necessary to prepare the minds of children to meet changes which are constantly taking place. Years ago the invention of new things and the expression of new ideas were considered sinful. The eyes of mankind were turned backward to look for the true forms of behavior. The golden age was in the past. But the theory of evolution has turned the eyes of mankind towards the future. It is important to teach the child to doubt, to test, to reach rational and sound conclusions." And he quoted Tennyson that there lives more faith in honest doubt than in half the creeds.

So said Rasmussen. Perhaps it should be said, however, that probably not all Danes share Rasmussen's views on Darwin. Some of them, like perhaps many Americans, do not know whether Darwin was a taxidermist or a tax collector and they go about their duties, as should all Americans, peacefully and pleasantly. But that is what Rasmussen said.

The other man whose influence Rasmussen and all Danes instantly point to is Bishop Grundtvig, whose long life was a light and a benediction to the Danish people. Many interests were promoted by the influence of this man, and Dr. Rasmussen in his quiet study on that dark January afternoon related, as most Danes delight to do, the services which Grundtvig performed for Denmark. He caught the imagination of the people as few leaders have ever been able to do. They sing his songs and read his books and quote his sayings in Denmark now, and in nearly every household in the land one may find his picture.

His educational influence was wide, but the folk high schools, already referred to as Denmark's distinct contribution to education, are, in ideal at least, but the length and shadow of their inspirer and founder, this "Prophet of the North." Histories of education tell little if anything of him or of his great work and influence in Scandinavia. But the Royal Danish Library in Copenhagen and the library in the University there contain scores of his own literary productions and quite as many more titles on his life and work as theologian, historian, patriot, poet, and educator; and distinguished was he in each of these capacities, even though his enemies accused him of false rhetoric. His long years of literary activities made him perhaps the most voluminous of all the Danish writers. Many are the eminent Danes who have left their impress on their fatherland, but few have had a more lasting influence in Denmark's history than this powerful, fascinating, documentary character.

Grundtvig was born in 1783 in a country parsonage in the strictest odor of orthodoxy, a typical child of the manse. He was fortunate both in ancestry, which included many distinguished theologians and scientific scholars, and in an upbringing in a home of high culture set in the midst of Zealand's natural beauty. Very early there seems to have been awakened in him, through stories and legends read to him by his mother, whose ancestry was renowned, a quite keen, even remarkable historical, religious, and literary sense and appreciation. And some of the lessons of his childhood prepared him to wage in the vigor of later life incessant warfare against ignorance and prejudice and civic unrighteousness. These he fought as he fought the many other afflictions with which he saw his countrymen suffering during the troublous times of the early and middle nineteenth century.

By 1821 Grundtvig was a parish priest, but he believed the Danish ecclesiastical system too rigid and frigid, and from that year until his death in 1872 he made battle, with apostolic fervor and the vigor of a militant crusader, against pharisaism, intolerance, and bigotry. This caused him to be viewed as an outcast in a protestant religious society which did not tolerate nonconformity. There must have been something primitive in his powerful character, for the intensity of his purpose made him a maddening terror to those whom he opposed. On the other hand he was, throughout his long and spectacular career, an object of almost idolatrous devotion to those who favored and followed him as disciples. Denmark had been languishing under a grievous ecclesiastical bondage of puritanical formality, and this he cried out against, only to draw upon his head all the fires of orthodoxy and sacerdotal narrowness. He had a passion for liberty and for those whom ignorance and religious formalism had fettered. There is some resemblance between his career and that of John Wesley, another crusader, who had finished his work when Grundtvig was only eight years old.

In the community where he received his first formal schooling, under the direction of a clergyman who served as parish priest in Jutland, Grundtvig first found sympathy with the underprivileged and the poor and ignorant for whom he later gave so much of his life. Until now he had lived in books. But in this atmosphere of the heath, which was so different from that of his home life during his first nine years, he met a different condition and it greatly impressed him. Here he spent six years in preparation for the Latin school to which all boys of his origin and station must then go. But there was opportunity also for travel and this made him familiar with and deepened his love for his native land, brought him in contact with its many dialects, and gave him such a knowledge of his own tongue as to make him later a master of expression, which he used to promote the welfare of his people.

Two years he then spent in the Latin school in Aarhus, two useless years he thought, and then he entered upon theological studies in the University of Copenhagen in deference to the wishes of his devout parents. The teaching here seemed as deadening as in the preparatory school. Only one teacher seems to have greatly influenced him and that was his own cousin, Steffens, whose free and spirited lectures captivated the youth, an influence which later appeared in Grundtvig's poetry. His theological studies finished he turned tutor, and soon met his first great crisis, an unfortunate because impossible attachment for the mother of the children whom he tutored. The experience served him badly for a time, but it and his patient attempt to forget the passion in a study of Goethe, Schiller, and Shakespeare, seemed to have awakened his poetic nature which, unfolding later, gave him eminence among northern poets.

Another crisis, religious in character, later made him a careful and reverent student of the Bible and of historic Christianity. He went straight to the Gospels, to the Lord's Prayer, and to the Sermon on the Mount, and in these he found the basis of a practical living Christianity. He gave the remainder of his years to an effort to establish it among the Danes. But Grundtvig was more than a religious reformer. He was a great nationalist, one of the earliest in Europe, and a violent but sincere partisan of Denmark against Germany and the Germans, whom the Danes do not love today. His writings, whether prose or poetry, seem so national in theme and purpose as to be quite outside and beyond the European tradition.

"Why is the Lord's word departed from His house?" was the subject of his trial sermon after his ordination into the ministry, an effort which inflamed the clergy whose unfriendliness followed Grundtvig the remainder of his days. It even led to his withdrawal from the pastorate of the church which his father had served and which he himself had assumed on his father's death. Seven years later he resumed the office only to withdraw again, however, for similar reasons. Some years later he returned to the ministry, this time to continue in it until his death at the age of 89, but he did not always have a place to preach except at the workhouse. In 1861 Frederick the Third made him titular bishop without a see, a circumstance which greatly vexed the real bishops who excluded him from all pulpits in their dioceses.

Twenty-two years earlier, in 1839, when Christian the Eighth had come to the throne, the poet-prophet had access to no state church pulpit in all Denmark, and this monarch appointed him chaplain to the workhouse where he remained as preacher until his death. It was this same ruler also who encouraged and helped Grundtvig, against the united wishes of bishops and government, to set up the folk high schools which have done so much and are even now doing so much for Denmark.

Grundtvig's services for the cause of popular education, for which he is so well known in Europe but scarcely at all in America, were the result of his efforts to awaken a slumbering people. It was a passionate effort. He early saw and deeply felt the need for an awakening from the effects of the defeat and humiliation of Denmark, following one catastrophe after another. Centuries before, Denmark had been mistress of almost all Europe. The conquering Vikings had pressed boldly, often even savagely, into new territories and set up new kingdoms. But Denmark saw herself going backward and losing her former place in the councils of European affairs while other nations were forming themselves into greater strength and power. The Danes had lost their cultural individuality. Even their language was being replaced by French and German as the medium of culture. The country had been reduced by the sword, the people were poor and broken in spirit, even before the crowning humiliation that came during the Napoleonic wars. Denmark had failed in her policy of neutrality and when she preferred Napoleon to England her fleet was taken and her beautiful city was bombarded and burned by Lord Nelson, who claimed not to have seen the signal of surrender. So, when Grundtvig was thirty years old his land was officially declared bankrupt and a year later, in 1814, Norway was lost to Denmark, after a union of four hundred years. The discouraged Danes listlessly expected complete extinction of their national life. National pride was dead. It was Grundtvig's task to restore it.

He had inherited and himself lived in the glories of a race which had a mighty past. The calamities and the evil days on which he saw his people fallen fired him with a zeal to awaken, to arouse, and to enliven his country and his countrymen—a spirit which they will now tell you in Denmark characterizes the schools which he inspired. To the mythology and history of the northern country he turned for inspiration. Would not the reputed traits of the old Norse gods serve to stir the drowsy qualities of his disconsolate people and awaken in them a sense of individual and national greatness? Were there not in their primitive history, in the glorious stories of Valhalla, and in the old Norse faith, evidences of a stalwart national piety which could even now be restored and strengthened?

From the Icelandic, Grundtvig translated Snorre Sturlason's *Saga*, from the Latin the *Chronicles of Saxo Grammaticus*, and *Beowulf* from the Anglo Saxon, works which gave him wide repute as scholar and author but failed to move the people for whom he thus labored. Through scholarship he had hoped to move, to influence, to change, and to improve the conditions which distressed him, but his confidence in the power of the press and of books began to weaken. The experience helped him no doubt to reach a definite point in his educational philosophy which was later to appear and which may even now be seen in the folk schools—that men learn best by living things and not by books. These attempts of his to modernize the classics of northern mythology, history, and poetry and to make the Danes familiar with their spiritual inheritance failed to stir their national spirit to energy and action. Grundtvig then turned to England where at Oxford and Cambridge he further pursued literary interests, during the fourth decade of the century. There he was impressed with an active political life, the reform legislation then taking place or beginning to take place, freedom for expression, for achieving experiences. These contrasts with conditions in Denmark sickened him. How could that country be made great and noble?

His literary efforts, wide and often brilliant, had been disappointing to him. He must leave the cloistered study and the quiet fields of scholarship if he would improve the condition of the people in the land he loved so deeply. There was no magic in the dead words of books, he was now beginning to say, but only in the living word of action among men. He would turn to a professorship in the University of Copenhagen, but there was available no post for him, perhaps a very fortunate circumstance for Denmark and the Danes. Through such a position he would have touched only a few people in comparison with those he later was able to inspire. An insulated university dais was then as now not the most strategic point from which a practical reformer of burning ideas and energy may clarify and give distinct form to the culture of the people, for then as now it was a veritable shelter for timid souls.

Another way to revive Denmark must be found, and this was in education, and in a type of education that was so real that it today distinguishes his country and illuminates and glorifies his own name in Denmark. The story of the origin, the development, and the present condition and work of the schools which he suggested and helped to build will be related elsewhere. But it is well enough to say here that Grundtvig's educational plan placed emphasis on inspired and inspiring teachers,—on men and women gifted with enthusiasm for that which is historically true, ethically noble, and esthetically beautiful.

"The revival of our country," concluded Dr. Rasmussen, who had talked so delightfully of Grundtvig, "had its origin in the teachings of this remarkable man. No preacher, or teacher, or politician, or industrial leader has so changed the course of a country's destiny as did this man, who was so often reviled. There was never a gentler, a more sincere, a more patriotic one. He lifted the poor of Denmark to a unique cultural level, heartened the underprivileged, increased educational opportunity, improved economic, social, and political conditions. The greatest need of the peasants of Denmark then was mental development, correct information, the habit of thinking and of thinking straight. And here is where Grundtvig placed emphasis. He led the people to seek the truth because he knew it would make them free."

Here is where emphasis needs to be placed in education in the United States. It is the emphasis now most needed here. And if a North Carolinian made bold to preach a bit on the timely text, he would say that the school and all other means of education worthy the name in any American state must give those who attend a safe and sound understanding of the things that lie nearest them,—of nature, and government, and of all those conditions which affect the welfare of the people now. If ignorance and groundless though deep-rooted prejudice are to disappear from the earth, the school must be made more fruitful for the people themselves and develop in them a rational and energetic love for the state and an understanding of all her various needs. Education must not fetter and bind men but release them from the graves and grammars of a dead and deadening past, and unite them in active, living relationships, through the noble and heroic of that past, to the pressing needs of today and tomorrow. Only this kind of education can develop in men and women sensible enthusiasm for good government and give hope and security for its future,—an enthusiasm, a hope, and a security which can be made real and lasting only through good teaching in every nook and corner of every state.

To say that Denmark of Grundtvig's time and any of the United States of today are altogether similar in problems and needs would be to press the parallel too far. But the problems of ignorance are always the same and always they require the same solution—enlightment. And some of the evils Grundtvig fought in Denmark, some prophet and crusader must eventually fight here. When he does appear he will be courageous and perhaps even bold, he will be true to conscience and to commonwealth, and bravely will he bid defiance to ignorance in all its forms, always and everywhere.

CHAPTER IV

THE MIDGARD SNAKE

SCANDINAVIAN children, steeped in Norse mythology and lore, like to relate the story of Thor, perhaps the most widely worshipped of the Norse gods, and his encounter with the Midgard Snake. This horrifying monster was one of the repulsive children of Lokè and a terrible giantess. He had grown so immense and had worked such mischief and misery that even the gods were afraid of him, and Odin, the supreme god, hurled him into the deep sea. There he lay flat on the bottom, grown to such a monstrous size that he coiled his scaly length around the world. Then one day Thor went fishing and caught something on his hook and when he tried to pull it in the earth quaked and volcanoes erupted. The serpent lashed the ocean into great sheets of foam and piled the waves mountain high, as he drew his long folds closer and tighter.

Thor failed to land the monster. And much later at Ragnarok, the Twilight of the Gods, the final destruction of the world, Thor fought his last great battle. Again it was with the Midgard Snake whose fiery eyes burned with revenge. In the furious combat Thor gained great renown by slaying his ancient enemy, but at the same time he himself was suffocated with the floods of venom which the dying serpent vomited upon him. The sun darkened, the earth sank into the sea, flames licked the sky, the glow upon the hills went out in blackness. It was the last sunset, and nothing remained but a vast abyss brooded over by a pale and colorless light. Ragnarok, the end of all old things, had come. But there was to be a regenerated world. A few of the minor gods survived the conflict at Ragnarok and Lif ("Life") and Lifghtasir ("Desiring Life") were preserved to repeople the earth.

Less than one hundred years ago agriculture in Denmark was in no better condition than it was in other European countries. Today Danish agriculture is perhaps the most highly developed and prosperous in the world and the Danish farmer ranks as the most scientific farmer of the present age. Denmark, when considered *pro rata* to area and population, is probably the greatest producer of agricultural goods that history has ever seen. Denmark and Danish farmers have reached this high development by three causes or influences: a favorable system of land tenure, scientific and well-developed methods of agricultural coöperation, and a close working relation between the theoretical agricultural scientist and the practical, dirt farmer,—a union of the college professor's laboratory and the farm itself. Energy has been combined with thought in Danish farming. Work on the farm has gone hand in hand with science.

Scientific education has contributed no less than coöperative organization to the success of Danish agriculture. The farmer in Denmark looks to experts in the numerous agricultural colleges for advice. Through them he and his sons, who usually become farmers also, have learned to a nicety, for example, just the kinds of feed for his cattle which will increase the butter constituent of milk. He knows his soil and its needs which he is careful to supply. And he loves his land. This knowledge and attitude he has acquired from the experts of the government experiment stations and the agricultural colleges and from the experiments reported in the farm journals which he reads carefully. And the love which he feels for the land which gives him and his family a good living is excited by the natural conditions of the soil itself. Fertility of the soil was not one of nature's gifts to Denmark. Within itself the land possessed little fruitfulness. Nor is it great in area. Those conditions appeal to the patriotism and intelligence of the Danish farmer who views the land as something to be cared for and improved. Intensive scientific methods have enabled him to make the land fertile; and science again, through the work of the Danish Heath Society, has reclaimed vast tracts of desolate land. Through this means trees have been made to grow in the heath which has also been converted into arable and pasture lands.

But the agricultural advance in Denmark has been made in very large part also by the system of small holdings. The great land holdings have been broken up by intelligent legislation which tended to parcel out the land of the few and put it into the hands of many. As already noted the condition of the Danish peasants was very bad until comparatively recent times. Legislation had improved their lot a bit in the eighteenth century. But until near the close of that century they were forbidden by law, enacted for military purposes, to leave the place of their birth from their twentieth to fortieth year. This gave great power to the large land proprietors to whom conscription was entrusted. The land remained in the absolute possession of a few very large landowners who let it out on very severe and oppressive terms to the tenant class.

About 1788, however, serfdom was abolished and progressive legislation tended to enable the tenants themselves to become owners of the land. By the middle of the nineteenth century further aid and encouragement were given by which tenants could buy land. Loan associations were formed by public spirited financiers and borrowing upon easy terms became possible. Many tenants bought from the impoverished nobility and soon demonstrated that the soil yielded much more when tilled by the owner than when it was worked by another. It became evident to large landowners that it was more profitable to sell than to cultivate the land by hired labor. Small holdings greatly increased as a result.

To hasten the distribution and increase the ownership of the land significant legislation was enacted in 1899. Other acts were later passed which revised, extended, and sought to strengthen the provisions of the initial law which laid the basis for one of the secrets of rural prosperity in Denmark. Before the act of 1899, however, savings associations had been formed among the Danes to encourage and aid people to purchase and own homes. Many such organizations have been formed during the last quarter century and receive assistance from the government.

Under the earlier laws the Danish government made provision by which the humblest hired man in the kingdom could buy a small farm and borrow on easy terms from his government the larger part of the cost price. A few savings and evidence of ability to care for and manage his own property set him on the road to home ownership. Under more recent legislation, especially that of 1919 and 1924, provision was made for the sale of the glebe or church lands, the conversion into free estate of fiefs and entailed estates and other lands held in trust, and the stipulation of the conditions which should govern the sale of public lands, all for the purpose of increasing small holdings. In the little more than a quarter of a century since its introduction, the modern small holdings legislation of the Danes has resulted in large benefits and much useful experience, and has acquired almost universal support in Denmark and attracted wide attention abroad. The Danish small holdings movement is a social endeavor of general interest.

The object of this effort of the government is to encourage and aid deserving young people to provide their own homes, to settle and live in the country, and to discourage their movement to towns and cities or to other countries. The legislation of 1899 bore the title, "A law concerning allotments for agricultural workers." Though revised and later extended it became evident in time that this legislation was inadequate to solve the whole problem, and further study led to legislation in 1919 which provided for the establishment of additional small holdings. The area of land made available under this recent legislation for this purpose was about 85,000 acres, which was sufficient for nearly 5,000 new small holdings Under the earlier legislation small holdings were acquired on private land purchased in the open market by loans from the government. Under the more recent legislation such holdings were to be acquired on government land. In the latter case the occupier is virtually in the position of owner, though he pays, however, no purchase money but instead an annual interest based on periodic valuations of that land, the government allowing loans on the buildings. These two features of the Danish agricultural legislation are to be retained for some years in an effort to ascertain which system offers the greater advantages to both the small holder and the government. The outcome of the experiment is being watched with great interest not only by Denmark but by other countries as well. The basic principle is that the small holding should be large enough to enable a farmer and his family to make on it a comfortable and satisfying living without the necessity of supplementing income by outside work.

Denmark aids prospective small holders by providing loans for them and also places at their disposal the advice of local government officials in selecting suitable lands to purchase. Under the legislation of 1899 a number of "parceling out associations" were formed by private effort for the purpose of acquiring and dividing up large areas and estates. These associations were intended to assist the prospective purchasers in the selection of farms and the raising of the necessary loans. There are about twenty of these associations. One of them has bought more than 120 large estates and parceled them out into nearly 1500 small farms, besides selling hundreds of acres to the government to be used under the land act of 1919. Another has helped to establish more than 1000 new farms. If the rules of these parceling associations are approved by the ministry of finance, they may receive loans from the government, using as security the estates to be parceled. They may also secure from the same source loans on second mortgages up to one-fifth of the assessed value of farms parceled out of such estates, if the value of buildings erected on such farms does not exceed 25,000 kroner (about $800). Government and private capital coöperate to remove and prevent tenancy and encourage people to own their farms and homes.

Under the old small holdings act of 1899 individual small farmers obtain aid from the government up to an amount not exceeding nine-tenths of the value of the holdings, that is, the total value of the land, buildings, live stock, and the necessary farm implements and tools. The loan value of the farms is every year fixed by the ministry of agriculture and the finance committee of the parliament; and a loan may not exceed the price paid for the land and the actual cost or fixed value of the buildings. Provision is made for the advance payment of a sum equal to nine-tenths of the purchase price of the land as shown on the registered title. When the buildings are roofed in, the holder, with the approval of the local officials of the government, secures a further loan on the buildings up to one-third of their value. These loans are secured by a government mortgage on the entire property and this cannot be terminated or foreclosed by the government so long as the holding is used according to the original purpose.

Interest at the rate of 4½ per cent is paid on loans on land. The same rate is paid on the building loans up to a statutory maximum. Any part of the building loan exceeding 800 kroner (about $2000) is free of interest. No installments on the loan are paid during the first five years; but after that time the interest-free part of the building loan is repaid in annual installments equal to one per cent of the entire building loan. After this part of such loan has been repaid the remainder is paid off by annual installments which include both the principal and the interest. These annual installments equal the original interest on the interest-bearing part of the building loan plus one per cent on the total of such loan. The loan on the land is finally redeemed by annual payments which equal $5\frac{1}{2}$ per cent of the original loan, principal and interest. By these arrangements the small holder is given ample time to meet his obligation. Applicants for loans who show that they have saved out of their own wages the amount necessary to meet the loan requirements are given preference over other applicants. This policy was adopted to encourage thrift.

The land act of 1919 operates in a slightly different manner. Under the act of 1899 land was to be purchased in the open market. Under the plan set up in 1919 land may be purchased only at the sales of the public lands taken over or purchased by the government under that legislation, for the purpose of providing small holdings in places where no suitable land has been available. To promote the operation of this new plan, the Danish government appropriates liberal sums.

Under this plan the small holder pays no purchase money, but obtains the farm against an annual interest payment of about $4\frac{1}{2}$ per cent based upon periodic valuations made by responsible property valuation committees of the government. Loans, not exceeding nine-tenths of the cost, are made by the government for the purpose of erecting suitable buildings on the small holdings.

Interest at 4½ per cent is paid on loans up to 8000 kroner ($2000), the remainder being free of interest. No installments on such loans are to be repaid during the first five years. Afterwards annual installments of one per cent on the entire loan, the interest-bearing and the interest-free parts, are paid until the obligation is fully discharged. A man with one-tenth of the amount needed for buildings and a sum sufficient to purchase live stock and provide a little working capital may obtain a small holding under the act of 1919. The right of preëmption is reserved for the state if the property is to be sold to any other than the direct heir of the original occupier. It is significant that this right has never been exercised by the government, according to reports.

Rather remarkable are the results of this land system of the Danes. The arrangements seem quite equitable. Under the plan of 1899 the number of new farms established or holdings obtained has reached nearly eleven thousand, aided by government loans and subsidies of nearly twenty-three million dollars. During the first four years of the operation of the new plan of 1919 more than 1800 new small holdings, nearly 40,000 acres, were acquired by government loans of more than six million dollars. These plans have encouraged thrift, decreased tenancy, and helped to make of Denmark a commonwealth of home-owning people. Small and medium-sized farms are the rule among the Danes. Large farms cover only a small part of the area. Legislation for a long time has sought to maintain the greatest possible number of independent farms, and throughout the present century positive effort has been made to establish new farms and encourage people to buy and pay for them. Most of the farms are protected by a prohibition against incorporation in large ones. Parceling is allowed, though there is a prohibition against reducing a farm below a certain size. Since 1919 a farm cannot be closed without the approval of the ministry of agriculture.

For the provision of small holdings very large areas have been and are still being parceled. The government expends large sums in this work, but only a small part of these funds can be regarded as public expense. Very little is lost in interest or by other means. Most of the money appropriated for this cause is carefully invested as loans against mortgage security in the small holdings and in time is repaid. The public appropriation is regarded also as a revolving fund. Against the comparatively small loss must be placed the large advantages that accrue to Danish agriculture in the increase of the number of its independent holdings, greater production and export, and in the increase in coöperative effort in marketing and in education.

The Danes are home-owning and education-loving farmers. Their desire for education finds root in the fact that they own their homes. The Danish farmers want their children to have better opportunities than they themselves have had. Most of the small holders are married men. If their families average five persons, the Danish small holdings legislation has made provision for as many as 75,000 people who might otherwise have left Denmark or gone from the rural to the urban areas to increase unemployment or other problems. To these and others Denmark has been able to open other doors of hope. Long ago the Danes learned the wisdom of getting the land into the hands of the many and of dissolving the most vicious and destructive of all monopolies, the monopoly of the soil. They turned to the task of converting themselves from tenants into land lords. In transforming their own conditions they have regenerated and reclaimed the soil they till and have made of Denmark a fruitful and happy agricultural community.

In Denmark one may hear some but not many objections to the land system. Occasionally there is heard a criticism of the law of 1919 which enabled the government to "take over" certain large estates against compensation. A visitor is likely to be told that injustice was not avoided in every case when a large estate was desired for small holdings. It was hinted that the process in some cases seemed confiscatory, but always the answer of the government would be that the end justified the means. In the main, however, the objections concerned certain details of the operation of the plans for establishing small holdings.

Some people believe, for example, that the amount which the applicant for a loan has to furnish is too small and that it may sometimes be difficult to establish whether he actually has the amount. They believe that the ninety per cent state mortgage is too large. One may also hear that the small holdings attract an inferior type of worker, that there is the temptation of the large estate owners to get rid of the worst land to the small holders, and that the small holdings deplete the large farms and estates of necessary workers. One may also hear that the cost of the land may often be raised by the natural operation of the law above the ordinary market value, the owner being likely to hold out for a high price when he knows that he is dealing with an anxious buyer whose funds are a loan from a rather benevolently inclined government.

In spite of these and other arguments, however, the plans for state aid in acquiring farms is credited in large part with raising Denmark from threatened agricultural bankruptcy to a position of security which has astonished the rest of the world. The Danish land system has become one of the most important economic foundations of Denmark's high level of rural life. The Dane owns his farm and works for himself.

Apart from the interest of the Danish government in promoting home and farm ownership by giving financial support to prospective purchasers, two other facts are significant in the small holdings movement. These are the coöperative organizations and the small holders associations. Coöperation in agriculture and in other interests has proved itself to be absolutely necessary to Danish life. Without it Denmark would perhaps be insignificant and attract little of the interest and attention which the outside world has had in that little country in recent years. Without it the small holdings plans could not have developed to that strength which amazes many other countries which have more natural advantages. In coöperation the common activities of a rural community,—farming, marketing, schools, libraries, and all other agencies of rural enrichment,—have been comprehended. It is of more than casual significance that coöperation was already established in Denmark before the small holdings movement began. In addition to the coöperative societies to which the small holders belong, they have also their own special organizations to care for their general economic and public interests. There are nearly twelve hundred of these local associations with a membership of more than eighty thousand.

The myth of the Midgard Snake varies somewhat in different ancient literatures. Scandinavian or Teutonic children know the story and relate it without any effort at interpretation. But the Danish adult has seen in it more than myth. There is allegory in it for him. The Midgard Snake is the land question, the Danish farmer will tell you. It is the question of all questions. When it is solved all questions are solved, say the Danes. They have hooked the Midgard Snake with much greater success than the old Norse god. It has made a great disturbance as it did on Thor's strange fishing party, but in the final combat the Danes triumphed. They know that peonage, peasantry, and tenancy, evils which once encircled Denmark and filled the the land with illiteracy and ignorance and squalor, did not pay. They united to remove these evils. Peasantry has passed, tenants have become their own landlords and masters, the curse of illiteracy has been removed, a new and better rural life greets an awakened people. Education has brought wealth to the Danish soil and health and happiness to those who live on it. It and they have been born again through education.

"The first and dearest work of this administration will be a supreme effort to translate the tenants of this state into landlords," said Governor Bickett to the people of North Carolina when he was inducted into office in January, 1917. He would attack the Midgard Snake, whose scaly and slimy length stretched around his state and so many of her sister states. He would scotch and kill it. To this endeavor he consecrated himself and pledged all the power and prestige of the high position he graced and filled so well for four years. The immediate problems which North Carolina's part in the World War pressed upon him interrupted many of his plans for reform, yet some of his recommendations were enacted into law during his administration. No problem in the commonwealth which he loved so deeply made greater appeal to him than that of the vast multitude of homeless people within its borders. To these he would open the door of hope.

That door has not been opened by any means, private or public. It has closed a bit tighter upon the tenants in North Carolina. When Bickett spoke in 1917, nearly forty-three per cent of all the farms in the State were in the hands of tenants. Today forty-six per cent are in their hands. They continue to mine the land and undermine the well-being of North Carolina, feeling no sense of guilt at the sight of a soil dissipated and wasted, powerless against the storms of their own ignorance, helpless in their own problems. The census data of last year show that North Carolina, with twenty-two million idle acres and a hundred thousand vacant urban lots that mutely appeal for the friendship and sympathy of man, is heading towards tenancy more rapidly than any other state in the Union. Every day the commonwealth grows a new tenant who "never hopes, with the emptiness of ages in his face and on his back the burden of the world."

The case is more or less the same in many other states. Between 1880 and 1920 tenant farms in the United States increased from twenty-five per cent to thirty-eight per cent. In the latter year the percentage of farms operated by tenants ranged from slightly above four per cent in Maine to nearly sixty-seven per cent in Georgia, with about forty-two per cent in Iowa and Illinois, twenty-four per cent in Minnesota, twenty-one per cent in California, and fourteen per cent in Wisconsin. The largest increases during these forty years appeared in the Southern, the middle Western, and the Lake Shore states. The official statistics show that during these four decades this country moved rapidly out of a land of home and farm ownership into a land of home and farm tenancy, with every geographic area, except the New England States, increasing its farm tenant ratios. Part tenancy now involves nearly ninety million acres and four billion dollars' worth in land and buildings; and full farm tenancy involves two hundred and sixty-five million acres and twenty-four billion dollars' worth in land and buildings.

The problem is most vicious and alarming in the South where the increase in tenancy since 1880 has grown from one-third of all farms to one-half now. In cotton and tobacco counties in some of those states nearly three-fourths of the farmers are tenants. The South today has two-thirds of all farm tenants in the entire nation, involving nearly eight million people. Moreover, contrary to what is believed, more than sixty-one per cent of the tenants in the cotton states are white instead of negro,—nearly 155,000 more white than negro tenants. In Texas four-fifths of all the farm tenants are white. The American farm tenant probably lives under the most vicious and wicked system of tenancy in the world. He is generally a short-term tenant and his contract is often not in written legal form. Half the tenants in the South move every year,—a restless, roving, and irresponsible element.

"Our immediate task is to rescue this tenant class," exclaimed J. W. Bailey, candidate for governor of North Carolina a few years ago, when he laid the problem upon the consciences of some of the people of the State. "It will never do to say that they and their children are destined always to be what they are. . . . We must not consign them to their fate. We must not abandon them. They are a part of the commonwealth. They are a part of us. They have a divine right to a fair chance. And we are divinely obligated to give it to them. . . . Manifestly we must take steps to encourage independent land ownership." And a plan such as that of Denmark or New Zealand he said he would like to see "tried upon a conservative scale under the auspices of the State." But not enough of the people were impressed with the idea to authorize Mr. Bailey to lead in that direction.

The Danes have learned that home ownership influences human character and that home owners take pride in membership in the community and have interest in its economic, social, and political welfare. They know, moreover, that farm tenancy is bad for the tenant and his family and bad also for the land they work, wearing it out and destroying its fertility. They know also that farm tenancy compels the one-crop system and prevents diversity in farm products, which is one of the best known remedies for adversity in rural communities. They have learned also that farm tenancy strangles education and intellectual growth, that it is one of the causes of illiteracy, that it breeds and cultivates undemocratic tendencies, prevents coöperative action, and hinders a wholesome political interest. The Danes placed the evils of tenancy and of hereditary landlordism upon the conscience of politics and statecraft. It may be necessary to do this in the United States, though that will be a most difficult task, because in most of these states conscience has no more to do with politics than with gallantry, to reverse a remark of Sheridan.

CHAPTER V

CHECKING THE WASTE

TWO essential foundations for the excellent educational conditions of rural Denmark are almost immediately apparent to the foreigner who views the schools there. One of these is economic prosperity in the rural sections of the kingdom. The other is a strong and natural antipathy or aversion toward ignorance and the correlative attitude of deep respect which the people have for sound learning. The tradition of education is long and strong among the Danes. They are ashamed of ignorance and stupidity and they seize upon every opportunity to increase their knowledge. These attitudes and habits are both the cause and the result of education in Denmark. Economic prosperity has been gained and promoted by agencies which have been inspired and encouraged by the schools, expecially by the folk high schools and the agricultural colleges. And many other agencies for rural betterment are the children of and closely bound up with these schools.

One of the many services performed for Denmark by the folk high schools and the agricultural schools since 1864 was that of heartening the discouraged people of Slesvig. This is accounted a distinct contribution to Danish life. It was not an easy task to keep alive the spirit of nationality during the dreadful times which followed the defeat of Denmark. Many people despaired of her future as an independent nation and believed that her days were numbered. The little country had stood alone against and had been crushed by the combined strength of Prussia, Austria, and the German Confederation. Her spirit was also broken. But the old Viking temper and energy became aroused under the blazing leadership of men like Grundtvig and the stimulation of schools. The new purpose was to make Denmark great, to restore the country to its former strength and happiness. The will of the nation to live was resurrected, and this manifested itself in many ways. The moving inspiration came to be: "What outwardly is lost shall inwardly be regained." With this as the motto rural Denmark has been able to make many conquests.

In the story of these conquests are lessons for the rural sections of the United States. It is a story of industry and of ambition, of splendid enterprise and of almost stubborn perseverance, qualities which are so much needed in rural America. They are qualities which have reclaimed for Danish civilization much that seemed forever lost. They are qualities, moreover, which could give the rural people elsewhere much that may now seem quite beyond their reach. These conquests of Denmark have been made not in territorial expansion. They have been made rather in the building of a prosperous and profitable agriculture, in the making of many kinds of internal improvements and developments, in the building of schools and other means of culture, in making enlightened social reforms and in the growth of an intelligent and progressive spirit which continues to radiate vitality and hope. They are conquests which need so much to be made by many American states, particularly by the Southern states, conquests, moreover, which any one of these states can make under enlightened leadership during the decades just ahead.

Elsewhere in this book something will be said to indicate how the fight for nationality had been waged in Slesvig after 1864, especially in that part which was strongly Danish in sympathy. This fight was led principally by the people themselves, by those who had been inspired and encouraged by the folk high schools, whose golden age followed the loss of Slesvig. This conflict was somewhat different from that waged by other nationalities in Germany. In Poland the fight had been made largely by the priests and the large landed proprietors. In Alsace-Lorraine the upper urban classes had united with the clergy in the fight for nationality. In Slesvig, however, the fight was carried on largely by the common people themselves. And so the blow of 1864, as severe as it had been, was finally to prove something of a blessing in disguise. It was to help put an end to excessive romantic and sentimental dreaming of the people whose country for some years prior to 1864 had had a period of recuperation. But after that date harder tasks faced the people and called for a new leadership, tasks which aroused and put into play again those traits of character which were to help save the nation.

One of these tasks was economic. It was clear to all who loved the fatherland, which had been so ruthlessly dismembered by superior force, that the economic foundation of Danish civilization must be made more secure. For one thing the thousands of acres of untilled lands, the heath, the moor, the bog, and the sand dune, so extensive and numerous especially in Jutland, must be reclaimed and put under cultivation to help shelter and feed the people of the torn country. One of the most important phases of the general revival movement soon to gain strength in Denmark appeared in the organization and subsequent work of the Danish Heath Society, set up in 1866 under the leadership of E. M. Dalgas, whose name is still praised throughout the kingdom for his patriotic services in the time of dire need. Others were associated with him in this work, the primary aim of which was national and in which there was no thought whatever of private gain.

Many were the original objects which this society sought to promote and on which it expended its chief energies. It undertook the intelligent reforestation of the heath lands and other areas which were not suitable for productive agricultural purposes. Denmark, like England and Holland, belongs to the most woodless countries of Europe. Fifty years ago the wooded part of Denmark was less than six per cent of the total area. Today it is nearly nine per cent and this increase is due to the work of the Danish Heath Society. Another purpose was to plant hedges for shelter and enclosures. This organization also began the hard task of draining the land and of cultivating the bogs and the meadows. It undertook to supply marl and lime to those areas which were deficient in these substances, to plan means of irrigation, to build roads, and to convert waste into fertile lands. Within three years the society completed eighty miles of irrigation canals with an irrigation capacity for thousands of acres which were freed of sour and stagnant water and extensively fertilized and planted. Today these canals are numerous and have a total length of more than 300 miles. Many of the sluggish and winding water courses in Denmark, which is only a few feet above sea level, were also regulated. Rivers were straightened and the height of their water scientifically regulated so as to reclaim for cultivation the bordering lowlands and marshes.

This work, which began first in Jutland, so much of which had been neglected and reduced to unprofitable agricultural areas, soon extended to the entire country, including the distant Faroe Islands. Prior to 1860 there were in North Jutland alone nearly 45,000 square miles of uncultivated lands, more than half of which has now been restored through the work of this organization, which has enlisted the coöperation of many people in Denmark. The heath farmers perform most of the work but always upon the expert advice and guidance of the society. The movement represents an interest for the people by the people themselves.

Today this organization for rural improvement has nearly twelve thousand paid memberships representing almost every walk of Danish life. The membership fees are small. The organization has received substantial sums by bequests from many well-wishers who know the value of its work in the nation. Every year also it receives a large subsidy from the government. In helping to reclaim the soil, to improve it, and to inspire respect for it, this organization has helped to make and keep Denmark a rich and beautiful land, richer and more beautiful than it has ever been. Fresh territory has been acquired within the boundaries of Denmark, barren places have been brought under productive cultivation, marshes and swamps and bogs have been converted into meadows and pastures, and opportunities have been provided for more people to live and to make a good living in their native land.

The Danish Heath Society continues its great work of reclamation and irrigation, because there is yet much for it to do in Denmark. Its latest reports show that it is even now engaged upon several hundred water course regulations and drainage and cultivation schemes affecting 40,000 acres. In this work of reclaiming a barren soil, private philanthropy and public appropriation have combined with the intelligence and patriotism of some of the ablest leaders in Denmark to perform a noble service for the country. By scientific means much soil has been remade and many people have thus been taught the improvability and the nobility of the common sod. The Danes now know that the essential wealth of a country springs from the soil. This they conserve and protect with conscientious care. They have learned to use all the land, to abuse none of it, and to treat it as something sacred. The Danes have learned this through the schools and the expert knowledge which the schools supply. Every Danish farmer knows exactly what his land requires. He seeks and respects scientific assistance, and for every crop which he takes from his land he returns to it the equivalent in fertilizers. Here again is another lesson for American farmers if they would have a prosperous agriculture and would see built upon it other agencies of welfare and progress. They should be taught, as the Danish farmers have been taught, to know their land and its needs. Some of it cries out to be reclaimed and much of it to be protected from ignorance and carelessness and slovenly methods of tillage. American farmers should by some means be taught many things they have never had sufficient educational opportunity to learn about the foundation occupation in every civilization. The right kind of schools and other means of education would provide that opportunity as it has been provided by schools in Denmark.

For schools have done this and many other things for the Danes. Education in Denmark explains the country's progress in agricultural coöperation. It explains the dignity to which the people as a whole have attained and the high regard which they have for culture and the cultural possibilities of agriculture. Denmark now has, according to the latest reports of the ministry of education, seventy-eight schools and colleges established and maintained principally for the people of the rural communities,—seventy-eight in a territory about one-third the size of North Carolina or New York, or one-fourth the size of Iowa. The chief incentive of the work of these—the folk high schools and their children, the agricultural colleges—was found in the necessitous times following 1864, times which brought forth also the Danish Heath Society. These agencies have made of agriculture in Denmark almost an exact science and of farming a scientific business. The Danes do not farm for show or for amusement, but for profit. The young men who are picked for places as students in the agricultural schools enter with confidence in the soundness of the teaching there, but they say: "Show us how to make farming pay, and how we may live happily and profitably on the farm." Even the demonstration farms connected with the agricultural colleges are made to return a profit, which is the best demonstration that can be given the clever young Danish agriculturalists.

Among other efforts of the Danes to check waste, to increase their knowledge of and skill in agriculture, and to secure to the farmers the greatest economic benefits, is the work of the so-called scientific control associations or societies, which are milk recording organizations. They occupy a very prominent place in the Danish agricultural system. They are Danish in origin, but the excellent results which these societies have achieved have attracted wide attention in other parts of the world, and Sweden, Norway, Finland, England, Germany, Holland, and some of the American states have copied the organizations in part.

Every Danish farmer may know precisely, through the assistance of these societies, the economic value of each of his cows and how each compares in that respect with the cows owned by his neighbors. This information is gained through the control societies, the object of which is the improvement of the records of the members and the keeping of an accurate account of every cow, with regard to the cost of her feeding and to the quantity and fatty contents of the milk which she yields. This control in the dairying industry is exercised by experts appointed by the societies who visit the farms regularly and make scientific tests. The frequency of these tests varies, but by experiments the farmers have learned that the milk should be tested every two weeks. This work calls for a close working arrangement between the farmer and the agricultural expert, and in this as in most of the activities of the Danish farmers the highly satisfactory results are due to effective coöperation between the experts and the farmers in whose service they are working. The results of all tests are entered into uniform record books which are kept by the control societies throughout the country.

This significant coöperation in Danish agriculture goes back to the middle of the last century when it had its modest beginnings; but real progress in the work began when N. J. Fjord, the well known Danish agricultural economist, invented about 1879 an apparatus which was capable of checking the cream contents of milk to determine its butter-yielding properties. In time the factors which determine the richness of milk were discovered,—the food of the cattle, the improvement of breeding. In time it was evident to the Danish farmer that it was necessary to give preference, for breeding purposes, to those cows which showed the capacity to yield rich milk.

The first Danish control society was formed in 1895 in Vejen, in South Jutland. Today there are more than a thousand of these societies in all parts of Denmark with a membership of nearly 30,000. Nearly 400,000 cows are closely observed regularly with regard to their net productivity of milk and butter. About thirty per cent of the dairy stock is subject to individual control exercised through these societies, though some parts of Denmark, Funen, for example, show a much higher percentage of their cows under control.

In the promotion of this work for Danish agriculture the central government grants to these societies annually a subsidy of more than $30,000. These grants are distributed by the minister of agriculture under appropriate legislation designed to investigate and promote the profitableness of animal husbandry on the basis of scientific tests of feeding and of milk yielding, and to promote the breeding of strains whose milk will give an increased butter yield. Every society must have at least ten members with a total of at least two hundred cows in order to participate in this assistance from the government, and it must, moreover, be incorporated under one of the coöperative organizations of the country. Detailed information is required for each cow registered in the society which receives state aid. These societies are formed like other coöperative organizations in Denmark, and are conducted by specialists highly trained through the agricultural colleges. In this as in all other parts of Danish agriculture correct information and knowledge have been applied to the problems of farming.

Nature has not done much for Denmark. So Denmark has been forced to do something for herself. By the application of knowledge to her problems she has been able to conquer many difficulties. If this little land, at odds with nature, can reclaim and make valuable vast areas which were once worthless, what could not the farming sections of the United States do, blessed as they are by nature, if they would only apply to their agricultural problems more scientific information and intelligence? The productiveness of the well-favored agricultural portions of these states could be increased and the ill-favored portions could be greatly improved, and thus could be laid a better basis for land-and-home-ownership, for better schools and churches, which are not likely to thrive in communities of nomadic tenants, now so plentiful in the United States. A life and program of collective action which has made Denmark a prosperous and happy rural community would work wonders for any rural American state. It would give the state more and better agricultural instruction, expert agricultural advice in every county in the state, medical inspection and advice for the thousands of rural children now largely neglected in this way, and it would give other things which the people have /not learned to believe in and to feel the need for and to support fully.

In Denmark the work of all such agencies for rural improvement is closely related to the work of the schools. Education in variety and abundance has made the rural people in that country perhaps the most intelligent rural people in the world. It has, moreover, broadened their sympathies without which the activities of reform agencies could not have been possible. It has helped to produce a type of mind which may not always possess expert knowledge in great quantities but a mind nevertheless which is capable of receiving and of profiting by such knowledge.

The Danish people respect knowledge. They do not scorn it. They seek it and are willing to be guided by it. The schools, moreover, have taught the rural people of Denmark to read. Besides scores of daily newspapers there are scores of journals and papers devoted to agricultural and rural interests. And the Danes love books; they love and appreciate art; facts which are reflected in the humblest homes. A reading people with minds open to new ideas and willing to listen to expert advice, with a spirit of enterprise that leads to experiment, and with a burning patriotism actively concerned with the prestige and well being of the nation,—these are some of the possessions the rural people of Denmark have gained from their schools. These same possessions rural Americans can gain also if they will. But they must have better schools and better teachers. Nothing else can ever bring such values to a people anywhere.

CHAPTER VI

A Folk High School

A TRIFLE more than an hour's railway journey from Copenhagen lies the village of Hillerod, in northwest Zealand. It is surrounded by very beautiful natural scenery. Apart from this there are two other rather notable objects which may interest the visitor to that community. One of these is the celebrated Frederiksborg castle which has helped to give the village, on the edge of which it is situated, the name of the Danish Versailles. It is one of the greatest and most important of the older Nordic renaissance buildings and one of the most distinguished of the numerous monuments of Denmark. It dates from the sixteenth century. It encloses picturesque court-yards and in the outer of these stands the beautiful Adrian de Vries' "Neptune Fountain," adorned with many statues; but these are copies because the Danes' near but once very unfriendly neighbors, the Swedes, carried off the originals as war trophies about the middle of the seventeenth century.

Within the castle is housed the national historical museum, established some years ago by a wealthy brewer and now maintained by the well-known Carlsberg Fund constituted of brewery income. And every time a Dane or another drinks a bottle of "Carlsberg Export" beer he promotes art, so a young professor's wife urged at dinner one evening. The castle church, which is now the parish church, was for a long time the coronation church of the kingdom. The other rather notable object of interest in this charming community one finds little about in history and nothing at all in the guide books. It is a folk high school, one of those unique Danish institutions which attract visitors to Scandinavia and are often referred to in notes on present day Denmark.

"Come in, for you are very welcome." It was the voice of an elderly gentleman and the words were those which one always hears on entering a Danish home or school. It was Holger Begtrup, the principal, or *Forstander*, as he is called in Danish. He was sitting at his desk in his study in the Frederiksborg Folk High School, one of the most famous of the newer of these institutions, which he had founded some thirty years ago. For many years he had been an instructor at the well-known school at Askov, in Jutland, the most renowned of them all, an institution which may be called the mother of all the others. Mr. Begtrup was just then retiring as principal at Frederiksborg. As he talked it was evident that his love was of educational principles and ideals rather than of machinery and method and procedure for which, it often seems, too many school people in the United States have a barbaric, often even savage appetite. He gave the impression of a man of learning, of infinite patience, and of rigorous intellectual honesty.

The last thirty-seven years of his long life have been active and devoted ones for him as teacher, principal, and manager in folk high school work, and they have told heavily on what once must have been a constitution of iron. But his mind was active and eager after all these varied labors for the enlightenment and encouragement of the rural people of his country. Ideas as distinguished from facts took the leading part in most of his conversation and comments. A view of him and his record as folk high school leader helps one to understand something of the influence of the type of school with which his name is so closely identified.

For, it should be pointed out here, the chief strength of the Danish folk high school depends, as is the case in all schools, upon the strength and drawing power of the principals and teachers. Mr. Begtrup was well-known as teacher of Askov, the oldest and most famous of all these schools, and there and at Frederiksborg he has taught many thousands of rural youth and has given perhaps nearly four thousand lectures outside the classroom to his people in Denmark. His library is filled with important books, many of them standard English works. Krak's *Blue Book* tells of his work as historian and writer. His Danish folk history of the nineteenth century, in several volumes, and his edition in ten stout volumes of the works of Grundtvig, on whom he is a recognized authority, testify to his varied intellectual interests and industry. Last year he gave sixty lectures to Danish settlements in thirty American states, a tour on which he was accompanied by his son, then a chemical engineer in New York, and now succeeding his distinguished father as principal of the school at Frederiksborg. The old gentleman told of his trip, which he has described in a recent book for his countrymen, and exclaimed his delight with America and especially with the "Grand Canyon, the greatest sight I have ever witnessed." Now he is engaged on a comprehensive history of the Danish folk high school movement in which he has himself been a brilliant leader.

Begtrup represents the older leaders in the movement. He is a man of good university training and interests. It is just this type of leader and worker who has made the folk high school influence what it has been, so effective in the life of rural Denmark. Not all principals and teachers in these schools have his ability and outlook and interest, of course, and it is for this reason that many schools have been established only to fail and to be abandoned after a short time. Those which have succeeded have done so largely through the personality and leadership of the principals. This must continue to be the story of the folk high schools. But the story will be different in the future, if the places of these older and admittedly effective leaders are not promptly filled, as they are forced by age to retire, by others who burn with the same zeal and have the same interest. These schools still have something to do, perhaps much to do. They will be able to do it in the future as they have done it in the past if leadership as needed is carefully recruited.

"We folk high school workers are more prophets than teachers," said Mr. Begtrup as he began to answer questions. He was leading the way to the dining room where the ever-present Danish *Kaffe* was to be served to the teachers and the principal's family and the visitor. "We depend upon the living word, from heart to heart, from soul to soul. We have no such disciplines or courses of study as you find in other schools in Europe or the United States. We live together with our pupils and talk with them. And we have no examinations."

To the folk high school people this is apparently a very definite program and full of meaning. To others, even to many Danes, it seems very indefinite and without much meaning, and to many foreigners it seems so vague as to be quite outside their understanding. One foreign visitor to these schools seems to see in the system, if system it may be called, something of a cult, something esoteric and hidden and to be understood only by the initiated. Here, moreover, is one of the points at which the schools have been attacked,—the indefiniteness of their work, their almost blind dependence upon inspiration ("the living word") in instruction. This is always safe enough dependence, of course, if the lecturers and teachers are able and well-trained and are really inspired and inspiring, as Grundtvig, Kristen Kold, Poul la Cour and others seem to have been. It has been such leaders as these who have given to these schools the influence they have had. But without such leaders the folk high schools are likely to become only broken lights of their distinguished inspirer and founder.

Very few people, however, have ever openly criticized these schools. Most foreigners whether English, German, or American, and especially the New England "school marm" type who has often come to view the folk high schools, simply accept them as remarkable for their originality and magical in their effect and influence. But it is likely that most of these foreigners, including the one now writing, do not always understand these schools. To describe to one who has not seen them what they are and what they are trying to do is most difficult. Writers generally conclude their descriptions by saying that "the work of these schools is of the spirit more than of the matter," or that "it must be felt rather than seen" to be understood and appreciated, and this kind of report has helped to give to these schools the color of mysticism. Many Danes think the folk high schools are positively curious, or perhaps it is safer to say that some Danes think so.

But there are very tangible things about these schools. First of all they are privately owned and privately controlled. This is one of the most definite and important features of the folk high schools. Usually the school is the sole property of the principal. Young Frederik Begtrup had just recently purchased from his father the Frederiksborg School. He thought the property worth about $50,000, as property is assessed for taxes in that community. This is the basis of quite a comfortable living for the owner and his young family, if the liberal attitude of the government continues and the rate of exchange gets no more unfavorable for the Danish farmers. This latter condition has recently slightly reduced attendance in many of these schools.

A folk high school may be owned by a self-perpetuating board of trustees. This is the case at the school at Askov, in Jutland, and perhaps it is true also of the International People's College at Hamlet's Elsinore, a school which Peter Manniche, one of the most fervid and capable of the younger apostles of the high school system, established after the World War with the rather ambitious object of "bridging the gulf of estrangement and suspicion which exists among the nations of the world." More shall be said later about this school. Now it may be stated that when the school was first visited, just about the time for opening the fall semester in 1925, the handful of less than fifty Danish, German, English, Ukrainian, Austrian, and Swedish students present did not look very promising as representatives of leagues of nations or world court jurists. But perhaps the rough edges can be worn off in time. A few months later these same students appeared more promising. Manniche has a good idea.

Another feature of these schools which is tangible and very important is the large and liberal government grants and scholarships which they receive every year, in spite of their private character. This direct support amounts to something like a million kroner which means about $225,000 at the rate of exchange the latter part of 1925. This is a rather substantial sum to be given to some fifty-seven schools distributed over a territory one-third the size of North Carolina. It seems all the larger in view of the lack of state control and of only slight state supervision, which at best seems only nominal. But it should be kept in mind that Denmark is now called a socialist government, though Danish socialism seems tame, almost conservative, when compared with varieties of socialism which rage in other parts of the world. There are people, however, who believe that Denmark is over-democratized. And after one has been there a few months it seems that the government must have agents out scouting over the kingdom to find causes to which state appropriations may be given. The tendency alarms many people.

Young Frederik Begtrup explained the basis on which state support is given the folk high schools. The amount which a school get depends upon the number of its teachers and the amount of teaching which they do. Some of these may teach half time, for example. Another basis of support is the value of school buildings. As much as one-half of the salaries of the teachers, one-fifth of the salary of the principal, which he himself fixes, and six per cent of ten per cent of the value of the buildings may be allowed. Indirect state support is in the form of scholarships which the central government allows the local governments to award to needy and deserving students who without such aid could not attend these schools.

The actual work of the folk high schools is described in another chapter. But in concluding this note on the administration of these unique institutions one very interesting feature may be cited. It was at a noonday meal with the students and teachers at Frederiksborg School that the personality and fervor of the principal appeared as the chief strength of the folk high school work. The ninety students, men from 18 to 30 years of age, were seated on backless benches at long, crude but clean tables, and these sons of the soil, rather unpolished, some of them uncouth in appearance, were served rice porridge and then a slightly sweetened bread with a fruit juice sauce. Both courses were substantial and sufficient if very simple, and the men consumed considerable quantities. Simple food and simple living, it might be noted here, form a tradition of these schools which has come down from the early days. Some of the features of the school life, particularly the sleeping quarters (all the folk high schools are boarding schools) seemed to suggest a Spartan simplicity and severity. Most of the students come from modest and often very humble homes and the aim of the schools is, above everything

A Folk High School 71

else, not to educate them away from their work and station. There must, therefore, be plain living and high thinking, though it is not clear how the one can always give the other. The students must be returned to their homes with a spiritualized view of life. A typical Danish folk high school in the winter, at any rate, would not be the place a tired Rotarian should select at which to spend a holiday or vacation.

As Holger Begtrup sat at the head of one of these long tables he appeared quite like an aged prophet. When the meal, which occupied only a few minutes, was finished, he arose and distributed the mail, locating each student as his name was called and sailing the piece to him, often many feet across the room, with uncanny accuracy. Then he walked quietly up and down between the tables and in a slow, veiled voice told the students the news which the morning papers brought from the vast world outside to their little world inside Denmark. Absolute silence prevailed.

As he reported to them the massacre at Damascus and the destruction of a Danish hospital there, the eyes of the men moistened, and there was further evidence of the intense love which every Dane feels for Denmark and for all things Danish everywhere. For a man of his age Holger Begtrup could not be called infirm, for his voice and his step were steady, but attention was drawn to his appearance of excessive seriousness. He looked serene, however, and admirable, with capacity for a friendship which would seem to lie quite within the grasp of all his students. He reflected sincerity and strength, those qualities which students everywhere should be allowed constantly to see for themselves in their teachers. His attitude was not of the schoolmaster, however, but of the house-father,—he looked patriarchal, prophetic. The frosts of nearly seventy severe Danish winters had whitened his scanty locks and time had furrowed shrivels into his cheeks. He looked like a troll from some old Scandinavian cave, like some Druid who had survived the ages and could not die. And then at some quick Danish word which he uttered the men at the tables arose, joined hands for a moment, and left to go about their afternoon duties with an air of devout benediction settled upon them.

CHAPTER VII

Adult Education

"WE do not know as much about enlightenment as we know about enlivenment," said a folk high school principal as he led the way through his school in Zealand one day in November. On the wall in the general lecture room he had just pointed out a large painting by a rather celebrated Danish artist, showing Isaac standing in an open field before the tents at sunrise waiting to receive Rebecca his betrothed coming out of the north. The principal said: "That symbolizes the rural people of my country waiting to be awakened and enlivened and enlightened. But," as he continued to quote the words of Kristen Kold, one of the most distinguished and influential of the earlier folk high school leaders, "we try to enliven first and then to enlighten, or at least to enliven and enlighten at the same time. This we think is right, for enlivenment is what is needed."

He had come to respect this principle, which did not seem to clash but rather to harmonize somewhat with the rather popular pedagogical doctrine of interest which is talked of so much in the United States just now. The principal had reached this view by working with people who could, he thought, receive no enlightenment before they had been enlivened. They were plain people, they knew little if anything about enlightenment, and they needed to be enlivened. He further agreed with Kristen Kold whom, along with Grundtvig, the folk high school people never tire of quoting, that the Danes must be enlivened before they can be enlightened. That seemed just another way of saying that people must be interested before they can or do learn very much.

The private nature of their administration and the public support which the folk high schools get in annual appropriations have been noted elsewhere. Other support is from students' fees. These range in the *karleskole*, the five months' winter session for men from November to March, from seventy-five to eighty-five kroner, approximately $20, for board and room and tuition. In the *pigeskole* for girls and women for three months from May to July the fees for the same services are somewhat less. The difference in charges is doubtless due to the difference in the operating expenses of the schools in the winter and in the summer months and should be taken as indicating favoritism. But a great favor could be done Danish womenfolks if somebody would invent a better-looking and better-sounding word for girl. Look at it: *pige!* The very nature of this word is defamatory, malicious, slanderous. Danish girls neither look nor behave in such a manner, although they greatly outnumber the men, except when they insist on several changes of husbands, a condition or characteristic which is to be noted in a discussion of the easy Danish divorce.

The report for last year shows that 2800 men and a few more women were in voluntary attendance at these schools. Enrollments vary from 40 to 150 at a school, except at Askov, the "expanded" school, which has a longer term and more students. When it was visited toward the end of 1925 it had above 300 students. The age of most of the folk high school students is between 18 and 25 years, which, by the way, is exactly the age recommended by Grundtvig as best for the work in these schools, which is practically the same today as it was in the days of this great leader. Many other interesting facts about these institutions and their students appear in the Danish *Statistik Aarbog* for 1925, one of the most complete handbooks of public information any government could possibly exhibit, but few of those facts can be included here.

The folk high schools of Denmark are for all the people, the whole people, whether rich or poor, city or country. But they are generally attended almost entirely by the rural population. Yet Denmark is now quite above forty per cent urbanized. In the main the students are the sons and daughters of farmers but some come from the homes of artisans, tradesmen, teachers and clergymen. The folk high schools serve the farming classes almost entirely and their work is closely related to that of the farmers though it is in almost no way vocational in nature. The close relation of these schools to farm life has undoubtedly deepened the sense of fellowship and common interests and interdependence of the farming classes. This is impressively one of the strongest of all Danish bonds at the present. It has been strengthened without provoking much if any agricultural class feeling or struggle in the kingdom. It is a bond which makes for a condition of freedom from those conflicts which in some American rural communities have been known to handicap spiritual and intellectual interests which so much need to be made the common possessions of all the people,

Even the distinction between rich and poor is no longer so wide in Denmark. The folk high schools, it is believed, have helped to reduce it. Professor Otto Jespersen spoke of this one afternoon in his study in that quiet and charming little village of Gentofte, out from Copenhagen. He reminded his visitor, however, that although this was true, Grundtvig's ideal for Denmark, "with few with too much and none with too little," had not yet been realized fully. "We still have in Denmark," said the eminent professor of English, "a few with much too much and some with much too little." But the democratic distribution of property and what Harold Westergaard speaks of as "the spiritual movements" among the Danish farming classes have created a fellowship which helps mightily to unite all of whatever class, profession, family, or income. And there are many people in Denmark who believe that this condition has been developed in large part by the work of the folk high schools, which were born for the rural classes and which have in turn served to awaken in them a consciousness of their own duties and responsibilities. But, of course, there are some people in Denmark who do not fully believe this.

How this has been done, if it has been done by these schools, and there is evidence on the matter, is a part of the mystery which a visitor can scarcely understand when he has seen and studied these institutions. The lecture is the principal method of these schools. History or popular historical lectures are given so as to exhibit faith in the common man and to emphasize the importance of freedom in all its aspects. But it must be kept in mind that the terms of these schools are brief and many of the students do not attend more than one session. Moreover, the instruction is carried on often by teachers whose training is not uniform, often rather nondescript, and measured by some standards it is often quite low. Certainly not all the folk high school teachers have the best academic and professional training available in Denmark.

When compared with the training possessed by practically all teachers in the gymnasium that of the folk high school teachers seems mediocre. This is not true of most of the principals who have had excellent training, generally at the university, most often in theology. Many of the teachers have been trained at the seminaries or normal schools which prepare teachers for the common schools, some have had training at the folk high schools, and some have had both. But taken as a whole (excepting those teachers at Askov) folk high school teachers in Denmark did not appear a very prepossessing group. The absence of a uniformly well trained teaching staff in some of these schools adds to the perplexity when one tries to find the secret of their influence.

At Askov, in Jutland, the oldest and perhaps the best school of them all, conditions appeared a bit different. The teachers and pupils were better-looking. These latter were more mature-looking also than students observed in some of the other schools visited. The young women students (this school has both men and women in all of its sessions, which are longer than usual, a sort of high folk high school) were very attractive. In one class in oriental history appeared some up-to-date enough to be wearing their hair bobbed, which was altogether legal and is orthodox enough even if it did seem somewhat anomalous in such a place. Here also the students were using textbooks and were observed taking notes during lectures, which were more or less different from practices generally followed in the folk high schools where the use of textbooks and the taking of notes are not common.

This seems to be a tradition which some of the earlier of the folk high school leaders gave strength to in their work. Kristen Kold is said to have objected to his students taking notes while he spoke. He insisted that it would isolate them from the important fellowship which is so essential in good teaching. As a rule the students listen to the instructors talk. At Askov also the library seemed adequate for the uses of the school. But even at Askov the library seemed not to be used constantly. The young instructor who pointed the way had to hunt the keeper of the key and unlock the room to exhibit the books, which could be made of service, if generally used, even by a folk high school whose motto is "simple living and high thinking." Good books, properly used, have been known to advance both of these ideals. When the absence of a library was noted at a school the invariable explanation was that books from the principal's private library could be used by any students when they desired them. But the point is that the typical Danish folk high school is almost a bookless school.

One day at lunch or *frokost* at Askov the principal, Dr. Jacob Appel, who was for several years Minister of Education in Denmark, was asked what the school was trying to do with the students. A visitor to a Danish folk high school can always depend upon invitations to several meals with the teachers and students during the course of one day. About 200 men students were present at this meal. The principal waved his hand over the group and in answer to the question replied: "We try to help them become socialized in the right manner." "What will they then do?" he was asked.

Many of them would return to their homes and become farmers or the wives of farmers. They had all finished the work in the common schools (folk schools), most of them had attended a folk high school for at least one term, and they had come to Askov for further inspiration and some study perhaps, because Askov more nearly resembles a formal school than any of the others. Some of the students would become teachers in the common schools, or in the so-called "free schools," a sort of private "free" school for those who do not want to send children to the common schools. There is just a bit of this attitude left even in Denmark. One principal of a teachers' college was found who engaged a private tutoress for his grandchildren, although there was a so-called model school operated in connection with the seminary or teachers' college over which he presided. Some of the students also become teachers in the folk high schools which depend in the main upon Askov for recruits to their teaching staffs. And Dr. Appel also pointed out that the first ministers to the Danish settlements in the United States received their training at Askov. Some Lutheran ministers from those settlements were in attendance at Askov at the time of the visit.

The Danish folk high school, therefore, has few of the traditional furnishings and articles of equipment of schools as they are generally understood. There are no elaborate buildings elegantly equipped and supplied with books and laboratories. Most of the buildings are very simple. Such a school means rather a group of undoubtedly consecrated and ardent leaders who are seized with an almost mystic inspiration for the task of enlivening country people. They seem indeed to have done this and continue to be able to do so.

Here is doubtless one secret of the influence of these schools. The students are considered members of the big family of the principal. He usually sits with his wife at the head of the central table in the dining room where the teachers and students come together on friendly and common ground. The testimony of many of the former high school students who have been questioned about the matter is that the frequent heart to heart talks which life at the school permits with the principal and teachers have had more to do with influencing and enlivening them than most of the lectures, though these are often effective.

The aim of the teachers is to make permanent in the students enthusiasms of the moment. The older of the teachers delight to tell about what one of Kristen Kold's pupils said to this teacher. It is a story one often hears in regard to the high school work. "I enjoy your lectures but I do not understand them," said the pupil. "You should not worry about that," Kold replied, "If we put drain pipes in the ground we must mark their places in order to find them again. But if we sow grain there is no need to drive in pegs, for it comes up again. You may be sure that whatever you have listened to with pleasure, what has found good soil in you, will come up again when you need it." Kold, who was the first real organizer of folk high schools in Denmark, seems to have been a sort of rustic blend between a Socrates and a Pestalozzi. Quick with native wit and a ready store of idiomatic Danish, seriously contemplating life and its persistent problems, understanding human character, very apt in illustration, consumed with a passion to communicate to others that which had brought light and help to himself, he was a great teacher and capable of relating his pupils in a vitally important spiritual fellowship. In this kind of teacher one begins to see an explanation of the strength of the folk high school and of its influence. After such leaders and teachers the folk high school teachers in Denmark today would pattern their work, in trying to unite simple and even frugal living with a culture of the mind and heart.

A detailed account of the work of a day's program at a typical folk high school cannot be included here. A word may be said, however, about some of the subjects. History is perhaps the most important lecture subject in the schools. Literature in a rather broad sense would probably come second in importance. Through these subjects the schools try to accomplish their aims, and they engage the visitor's attention promptly.

But the work in music and song and gymnastics and physical education engage it also. It is a delightful experience to hear the students sing hymns, ballads, folk songs, and patriotic songs. All of them sing and most of them sing well. Music is an important subject in all Danish education and life. The people live in part by it. Then the visitor should go down to the very plainly but sufficiently equipped gymnasium and watch the work in gymnastics and physical training which all the schools stress, every day, for all the students, under expert direction. He will notice how it makes out of the most awkward and shuffling of the country bumpkins sturdy, clear-eyed, keen-witted men of really quite attractive bearing. Or he would watch Mrs. Appel, at Askov, herself a grandmother but who moved around as if she were a young student herself, lead the drills for the girls.

Most likely the visitor would have seen Mrs. Appel lead the music at the early morning devotional exercises of the famous school and still later busy herself with numerous other useful duties. But the work of Mrs. Appel which would doubtless attract the visitor's closest attention and hold it longest would be found in the gymnasium of the school where sixty or more young women do their systematic exercises,—attractive girls, full of healthfulness and of life, proud of their strong and beautiful bodies. The effect of this part of the folk high school work is far reaching. These young people, both men and women, learn to love play and physical recreation and they return to their home communities to organize gymnastic and physical exercise associations.

The visitor, if he happens to come from a typical American college community, is likely to be impressed with the sensible Danish plan of physical education and see in it many lessons for school and college youth in the United States. He will likely be made to see that in the United States too much emphasis is placed on developing specialized teams for competition in inter-scholastic and inter-collegiate contests and not enough on providing adequate physical education for all the students. Even college and university presidents have been known in recent years to speak out against this increasing evil. They should see the Danish plan, if they need further proof of the inadequacy of organized athletics in their own institutions. A view of a gymnastic class of Danish girls, for example, would be quite sufficient to enliven such educators and perhaps it would enlighten them as well.

CHAPTER VIII

THE ENCHANTER OF THE NORTH

IF ANY who may read this should ever by any chance journey from the northwest coast of Jutland, across that peninsula, on a cold winter's day, intending to pass on to the island of Funen, thence to Zealand by nightfall, all the way on a hard third-class bench of a slow Danish railway car, and with no chance whatever to get anything to eat until the ferryboat at Nyborg is reached,—the ambitious plan should be abandoned. It should not be undertaken in one day.

The strain is too great on the disposition. It is better to stop off at Odense, have the ticket validated by the station master for a later train, and spend an hour and a few kroner in eating one of the tastiest dinners to be found anywhere, in the most satisfying dining room of the whole Danish kingdom; for so it should be written of the Grand Hotel, in that charming little city of about fifty thousand souls, in this lovely little island, one of Denmark's many gorgeous gardens.

The high state of agriculture in this rich and fertile country, its scientific methods, intensive farming, numerous coöperative farm agencies, libraries, folk high schools, and schools in farm management and housewifery for the sons and daughters of the farmers, would captivate rural social-economists. And the altogether delightful life all around in the country would rejoice the hearts of eager supporters of improved rural conditions. Funen is one big smiling garden of rural peace and plenty.

But it should be confessed here that it was not the agricultural and educational prominence of Funen which engaged the entire attention of one visitor on a December day. It was Odense, perhaps the most venerable place in all Scandinavia, whose antiquity is so remote that Odin is popularly believed to have been its first mayor. But it was not Odense as the legendary birthplace of this supreme deity of Norse mythology, that one-eyed man with hat and staff; nor Odense as the scene of the murder of King Canute at the altar of St. Alban's church to which he had fled to escape his pagan pursurers, in the latter part of the eleventh century, when the town first got its name in history. It was not Odense whose wealthy families, according to the traditions of the place, entertained with much princely pomp and showed their contempt for wealth by burning cinnamon instead of wood on their hearths, when Copenhagen was yet a second-rate fishing village. The city did not attract the attention of the visitor because of *Klokkedybet*, the hole of the bell, that fathomless depth in the river into which, tradition also says, a bell flew from the church tower many ages ago and even now tolls beneath the water when a rich citizen of Odense is about to die. Nor did it attract as the cultural, commercial, agricultural, educational, and traffic center of this part of Denmark, but as the birthplace of Hans Christian Andersen, the enchanter, first of the north and then of the whole world, by his charming fairy stories. It seems so very fitting that a city of such hoary memories and traditions, so rich in Danish legend, should be the birthplace of him who was to open so many eyes to the glorious mysteries of fairyland.

Here one may learn afresh the story of his life and of that distress which arose from his own poverty and obscurity, ripened his soul, and led it through the world of dreams. Through the distress and the dreams of the child came those incomparable fairy tales which exposed false pride, extravagant luxury, empty pretense, and extolled and applauded the virtues of the honest and the humble; and as delights for children and for grown-ups have been victorious for nearly a hundred years. Their popularity increases. Scarcely a year passes without bringing with it a new edition or translation. In Odense one may see where their author lived and struggled in his youth.

On the hundredth anniversary of his birth in 1805 the council of the city erected in his humble birthplace a museum to the memory of the famous son. There are other memorials to the great writer here, but it is the birthplace which has most interest. The house is in part restored to the shape it had when Hans was born there, the son of poverty-stricken and somewhat shiftless parents, though his father was a great reader and inspired in the boy a love of books. One needs no deceiving elf of illusion in attendance at the place. It requires but little effort of fancy to reconstruct a vision of Denmark in the early part of the nineteenth century when Hans Andersen first saw the light of day. The house is in an old, narrow and winding street not yet invaded by the modern in architecture. The surviving structures are very poor, phantoms of antiquity. Here, if anywhere in this northland, the spirit of beauty and of fancy should be allowed to linger, untouched by the ruthlessness of the years. For here, from the

BIRTHPLACE OF HANS CHRISTIAN ANDERSEN IN ODENSE

bottom of the house to the tiny little garret windows in the gabled roof, are all of Andersen's personal effects that could be collected from wide circles,—the figures and pictures he cut as a child, the keep-sakes of his hopeless love in his youth, manuscripts, letters, furniture, clothes,—and they all seem to speak the fairy tale of the odd master whose own life was such a beautiful story.

It was a cold and snowy day, or night—because it is quite dark by four in the afternoon anywhere in Scandinavia in winter—and the frost lay in icy blossoms on the window panes. The chill wind shrieked as it swept past the corners of the old house, under whose low doorway thousands every year bow their heads in order to pass into the precincts which are so closely associated with the great master of story-telling and lover of children. And one is reminded of another great debt which the world owes to little Denmark for the gift of Andersen, who is known and loved wherever there are "ugly ducklings" and people young enough to follow him in his fantastic and whimsical adventures.

In Odense they say that he was far from a good-looking man. Those who knew him were impressed with the ugliness of his face, which was that of a peasant; and a long life of close association with people of culture and education, of keen sensibility, did not remove from it the stamp of the soil, they say. He was very tall and thin, had long and swinging arms, huge, ungainly hands, ugly nose and mouth, and his manners were clumsy. He seemed to provoke merciless laughter among adults and to fill children with fright whenever he came around them. His ugly and awkward appearance constantly brought him great distress.

But they will also tell you that any unfortunate impression which one gained of him passed away as soon as he spoke. His eyes were small but there was something of sweetness and vivacity of expression in them, and gentleness breathed from everything he said as it did from everything he wrote. He must have possessed great inward distinction, for the man of genius stood revealed in his smile, and in his spoken as in his written word. Men and women, they will even now relate in Odense, in Copenhagen, and in the country communities, have many times over testified to their experience as children in his presence, when all sense of shyness and reserve fell away and they were made to feel comfortable, and to talk freely with him. He made many children happy as he read his stories to them. Nature herself must have blushed with sheer ecstasy at the sound of his low whispered voice, as he read a new fairy tale to his young friends.

Everybody seems to have loved Hans Andersen and all Danish homes were always open to him. One of these was his second home. It loved him and he loved it very much. A constant welcome awaited him at *Rolighed*, the name of this home, a word which in Danish means quietness, tranquillity, peacefulness. Three or four of the charming rooms were set aside for Andersen's exclusive use and he came and went at will. In a poem which he called *Rolighed* he wrote with tender gratitude of its hospitality, calling it "My home of homes, where my life regained its sunshine and my harp its tone."

Andersen was admired and loved by the English and the Germans as much as by his own people. In Germany last year there was a rather significant celebration and exhibition in honor of his life and work. In England and the United States interest in his stories continues to grow. And he had great affection for the English among whom he always met with a most hearty welcome. Quite early in his literary career he rejoiced over the warm appreciation of his English critics "who seem," he wrote, "only to look upon what is good in my writings." Among the eminent English writers who greatly respected and admired him were Charles Dickens and Bulwer Lytton whom he counted among his best friends. And, it may be recalled, Andersen supplied the theme for Elizabeth Barrett Browning's poem *The North and the South*, the last lines the gifted woman ever wrote. She had met him in Rome in 1861, only a short time before her death. In that poem she pays a great tribute to the Danish author:

"Yet oh, for the skies that are softer and higher!"
   Sighed the North to the South;
"For the flowers that blaze, and the trees that aspire,
And the insects made of a song or a fire!"
   Sighed the North to the South.

"And oh, for a seer to discern the same!"
   Sighed the South to the North.
"For a poet's tongue of baptismal flame,
To call the tree or the flower by its name!"
   Sighed the South to the North.

So the North sent therefore a man of men
    As a grace to the South;
And thus to Rome came Andersen.
—Alas, but must you take him again?"
    Said the South to the North.

Two of Andersen's stories, *The Cripple* and *Auntie Toothache*, readers of this are likely to recall. They come to mind as one moves about in his old birthplace here in Odense. The stories cannot be given here, because the North Carolina newspapers in which these notes appear are not in the habit of printing fairy stories except during the campaign seasons. Perhaps a word may be said, however, about *The Cripple* which presents so well Andersen's great lesson, his imaginative message to mankind. In it, too, may be seen something of Andersen's own life, his high respect for values, his eagerness to discriminate between the important and the unimportant, the real and the unreal in human life and civilization. *Auntie Toothache*, which ends his long list of beautiful fairy tales, seems to have been inspired by his own drastic sufferings. One of the stories a Dane even now is fond of relating to a visitor who has more than a passing interest in the great writer, tells of Andersen's first appearance in Copenhagen, poor, forlorn, and without sufficient money to buy a single meal. He himself wrote: "I spent the few pence I possessed to obtain from a library one of Walter Scott's novels and reading it forgot hunger and cold and felt myself happy."

The Cripple is not one of his best known stories nor one of the most characteristic. It contains not much of the fantastic or supernatural. It is a little but somewhat complicated episode of humble manners; and in the story, which is also a sort of *Apologia* for his long poetical career, he tries to defend fairy stories and their writers. More important, however, is the theme itself. It tells of a gardener and his wife who had five children. Hans, the oldest, was a bedridden cripple. The parents were good and worthy people but lived close to the soil, absorbed and engrossed in materialistic interests. At Christmas the people of the manor on which the gardener and his family labored gave presents to their workers. Hans received a book of fairy stories and his parents very ungraciously said: "Our boy cannot grow fat on that." But the stories awakened Hans' whole spiritual life. Among them two very simple and direct parables,—the story of the woodcutter and his wife who complained so much of their lot and were ungrateful, and the story of the "Man without sorrow or need"—were read many times by Hans to his parents as they came in complainingly from their work. In due time they also were moved by the tales, and their hearts became humanized. The mistress of the manor later gave Hans a little bird in a gilded cage. One day when he was all alone a vicious cat tried to capture the bird; and Hans in his supreme effort to save the bird from danger and destruction regained his own strength and found that he could walk. In the end,—but the story should be read if it is not known.

Hans Andersen performed many services for Denmark and the world. Not the least was the interest which he aroused in reading. This is a service which many people in the United States need so much today. Andersen's influence in this respect is still felt in Denmark where there are many eager readers and lovers of books. The contrast between the Danes and Americans in this matter of books and reading is sharp. When this was written North Carolina newspapers were bringing reports of the meeting in Chapel Hill of the Library Association of North Carolina and another reminder of that state's low rank in libraries and in people who read. The association recognizes the situation as deplorable, the headline of one paper stated, and then it goes on to tell of a resolution recommending a campaign of publicity and activity to help raise the state of denim mills, tobacco and cotton factories, hard-surfaced roads, and one hundred thousand native, white, adult illiterates, from the humiliating 48th place with fewer public library books per capita than any other state in the union, which probably means anywhere else in the civilized world. Here the late Charles B. Aycock of North Carolina could not give thanks for South Carolina which kept from the bottom his own state, which is the poorest book market in the United States, with fewer libraries and books and a larger non-reading population.

Some of the facts brought out in the meeting seem to have startled the librarians themselves. They should be dinned daily into the ears of every teacher and preacher, every editor, every other citizen in the state and often every day into the ears of all the statesmen who want to go to the legislature. When the writer read the statement of those facts he studied the statistics on Denmark. Public libraries in this little land, one-third the size of North Carolina and with only a few more people, number nearly eight hundred with eleven hundred thousand volumes and borrowings of nearly six million books a year. This does not include the Royal Danish Library with a million volumes or the University of Copenhagen Library with half that number. Moreover, local and state government annual appropriations for public libraries alone in Denmark are quite above two million kroner, which means more than a half million dollars. In addition there are 300 daily newspapers, and scores of magazines, and a bookstore on almost every corner in the cities and country villages. The Danes read.

The resolutions of the librarians, as noble in sentiment and purpose as they are, cannot alone remove North Carolina or any other American state from the deplorable position it now occupies. They will help, if the libraries follow them up in many ways. But the problem must be attacked on another side. Some day it may perhaps occur to the leaders in those states whose people do not read that reading is a habit which for most people must be built by the schools, if built at all. The major considerations of most Americans are still, in the nature of things, of the processes of getting and spending. In such processes they may lay waste their powers if deeper interest in reading and in learning is not aroused and sustained by the schools.

Reading habits are never developed and grown in communities of bookless homes such as now abound in the United States, especially in the Southern states, homes filled with non-reading members who are so fully absorbed in purely materialistic or empty interests. Some day it may also occur to somebody in those states that the concern of the governing authority in education should be not only for those who cannot read, but also for that larger army who may not even now in the schools be learning to read and to love to read. There should also be concern for those who can read and who do not. Somebody may even learn that children cannot be taught to read nor can reading habits be built in them by teachers who do not themselves read and are therefore unable to inspire in others a love for reading.

Better teachers are needed. It is the one big need in most American communities. A good teacher for every child could in time make of every state a community of libraries and of readers. Nothing else can ever work the transformation. If a state, crippled like little Hans in the story, ever saves itself from the fearful dangers that lurk among people who do not read, a supreme effort must be made to provide better and more extensive educational facilities. Only such an effort can give a community renewed spiritual energy. The effort will cost money for longer and better school terms and better teachers. The money must be provided by taxes. These must be authorized by the legislature. This is composed of politicians. Too many of these have too long been telling their constituencies that a free people fatten not on books and libraries and reading, on better schools and better teachers, but only on reduced tax rates. And these rates must be promised low by aspiring lawmakers many of whom, in too many American states, could never get to a legislature on any other platform.

CHAPTER IX[1]

SLESVIG AND NATIONAL MINORITIES

ONE of the most interesting educational questions in Denmark at the present is that of schools in Slesvig, that part of South Jutland which borders on North Germany. It is, however, more than an educational question. It is also a national problem and one of some danger to Denmark because of its very smallness. It should be of interest to other peoples inasmuch as there is involved in it the rather puzzling question of treatment of national minorities.

In January, 1864, the president of the Danish council announced amid loud cheers: "We are about to fight to prevent a foreign power from forcing itself into Slesvig." Prussia and Austria had united in war on his country, both had declared that they had no desire to dismember Denmark. The defeat was complete. The only spark of success that came to the Danes was in the naval battle off Heligoland in May. England's negotiations, during a brief truce, for the purpose of stopping the war, were as futile as they had been languid. Hostilities were renewed in June; and Denmark, hoping for help from Sweden and other powers which had guaranteed her integrity, was doomed to disappointment. The disaster which was overwhelming was followed by Denmark's relinquishing the southern part of Jutland. She could do neither more nor less. About 200,000 Danes were transferred against their will to Prussia

[1] The substance of this and of the following chapter appeared in *Current History Magazine*, for August, 1926, and is used here with the permission of the publishers.

and the German language forced upon them, Denmark being compelled to consent to these terms of the peace. In August the king of Denmark in a poignant speech to the Parliament said: "Since all Europe leaves us helpless, since we see ourselves obliged to yield to numbers, we must endeavor to close a war the prolonging of which would merely expose our beloved land to greater misfortunes and a still worse injustice."

The Danish population which thus came under German rule hoped that their subjection would be temporary only. It was a national hope and there was a legal basis for it. For in the fifth paragraph of the Prague Conference Treaty of 1866 there was a clause which gave the northern districts of Slesvig the right to decide by vote of the people to which nation they would belong, Germany or Denmark. In 1869 the Danish government opened up negotiations with Bismarck with the promised plebiscite in view but the effort availed nothing; and a few years later the wearisome article was arbitrarily annulled. It was not until February of 1920 that the election was held, under the provisions of the Treaty of Versailles, which was to rescue a large portion of the Danish people from continued subjection to foreign rule. The result was that northern Slesvig voted by a large majority to reunite with Denmark and the almost completely Germanized southern part voted almost as strongly to stay with Germany.

The rules of the election were obviously quite adroitly drawn, and they proved to be almost as good an example of practical politics as if they had been formed by some electoral geometrician in some Southern state. Only those people born in the territory affected by the election were

SLESVIG AND NATIONAL MINORITIES   97

allowed to vote. This territory was divided into two zones. The first comprised the northern part of Slesvig where the majority of the population was presumably Danish-minded; and the second comprised the southern part the majority of whose population was presumably German-minded. It should be recalled, however, that probably as many as 60,000 Danes had emigrated from northern Slesvig during the previous period of German domination, many of them to the United States, and these could not return to vote. But nearly all of the children of the large army of German officials, army officers, private soldiers, policemen, judges, teachers, clergymen, and the like were discovered and voted for Germany in communities where many of them had passed only a few years of their childhood. In one parish, for example, eight clergymen had succeeded each other in a very short time. Each had been married; and a rather large group of clerical children, now grown of course, cast votes for Germany. The story is also told on good authority that in one village there had been some gypsies for a short time years before, and a child was born to them. By 1920 the child had grown to an elderly woman but she was located and voted for Germany.

The Germanizing of Slesvig had gone on in many ways. By degrees German services were introduced into the churches and about 1888 Danish lessons had been abolished in the schools. Danish clergymen and teachers were dismissed and Danish private schools were forbidden. There was much emigration of young men to avoid the detested military service and foreign rule. The normal increase in population fell and by the early nineties north Slesvig was almost destitute of young men. When, however, the people fully realized that such a policy meant complete abandonment of their native land to German immigration and influence, they determined to remain and to try to preserve the Danish language and culture. For years they had hoped almost against hope that they some day might have their right to reunite with the mother country.

To stand by meantime, however, required much courage on the part of the people. Until one has talked with the Danes, in city or country, it is almost impossible to understand the agony this small but self-respecting country must have endured to hang so long over the brink of annihilation. In 1864 the demand of Prussia had been that Denmark should join the North German Confederation, which would have been to Danish national spirit worse than death and destruction by the sword and torture. By draining and draining again the resources of the little country the rulers of Denmark had been able to keep Germany at bay for a while, but for only a brief breathing space. Denmark's portion during that time was unspeakable sorrow. The portion of the Danish-minded people in Slesvig after 1864 was quite as painful. For all these years they have had to encounter many devices to Germanize everything Danish there, and, with the help of the school and the church denied, the task of resisting seemed hopeless.

But the folk high schools in Denmark helped in the solution of the problem. These were forbidden in Slesvig and parents were not allowed to send their children across the frontier into Denmark so long as they were within the age prescribed by the German law for school attendance. But many continuation schools grew up north of the border and to these were sent young Slesvigians above the legal school age, for instruction in Danish history and language. These continuation schools were in reality the children of the folk high schools whose former pupils had set them up and conducted them. Meantime, also, some few young people from Slesvig attended Danish folk high schools which had increased in number. But not all of them were able to attend. To meet this need a society was formed in 1892 to help pay the expenses of deserving pupils; and although Germany used severe methods to prevent it, the attendance greatly increased.

It was through this means, then, that the discouraged people of north Slesvig largely kept up their courage and renewed their strength. The folk high schools gave them greater faith in Danish culture and more zeal to see it restored. This is counted among the many fruitful influences of these unique institutions. Several thousand of these young Slesvigians attended these schools and the continuation schools between the foundation of the aid society and 1914. They returned to take a prominent part in the affairs and life of their communities. All the north Slesvig representatives in Berlin in the years just before the World War were former pupils in these schools as were also the members of the Reichstag and the Prussian Diet from this region. And the four delegates of Slesvig to the Peace Conference in Paris had all attended the folk high schools and the extended high school at Askov.

The place of language forms one of the most interesting aspects of the whole Slesvig question.

Perhaps the most important fact in the history of the problem is that many years ago church services and school lessons became Danish in north Slesvig and German in south Slesvig. But all of Slesvig, it should be kept in mind, is Danish in origin. The dialect of South Jutland is not only pure in its Danish genuineness, both in grammar and vocabulary, but many of the words in use there are of ancient origin, quite vanished from modern Danish but still found in Norway, Sweden, and Iceland. The Slesvigian dialect is almost pure Scandinavian.

A terrible ordeal to the people of Slesvig was the World War which claimed as sacrifice six thousand of their young men, just twice as many as were killed in the war with Prussia in 1864. These soldiers were German subjects. They fought foreign powers against which they had no enmity or bitterness. It was a severe test of their loyalty but there is evidence that it never wavered. And the letters which these soldiers wrote home during the struggle are a unique literature of the war,—letters written in Danish, the language of the land they loved, from which they and their parents had been wrenched. Few, if any, of these soldiers had ever received a single lesson in Danish at the hands of the government which they now defended. The spirit of the letters was also Danish and bore the tone of the will to surrender all for those at home. It was in the folk high schools and the continuation schools that these soldiers had learned to keep alive the language of their old homeland.

It may be recalled that in 1848 the German-speaking population in Holstein and Slesvig revolted against Danish rule. The insurrection was put down by the Danish army and, in order to preserve the Danish language and culture, provision was made that half of the church services and most of the school work should be in Danish in those parts of north Slesvig where Danish was still spoken either by all or by a part of the inhabitants. This action of the Danish government was not considered altogether benevolent or wise by some, and many otherwise loyal people of Slesvig became adherents to the German movement. If the Danish government had given the people a free choice between Danish and German, the subsequent story of that community might perhaps have been different. This interesting point is here noted because the present policy of Denmark in dealing with the German minorities in that portion of Slesvig which was returned to Denmark in 1920 is a very liberal one.

There are now, therefore, two national minorities in this territory, a German minority in north Slesvig and a Danish minority in south Slesvig. All Danes and perhaps all other Scandinavians are agreed that Denmark did not recover too much of south Jutland in 1920. Many Danes regretted to lose to Germany any of south Slesvig, especially the thriving little city of Flensborg, on the frontier, which by a diplomatic fiction had become German years ago but which would doubtless be Danish now if the fifth article of the Prague Treaty had been observed. And all Danes, so far as one can ascertain, especially that heroic Danish minority in south Slesvig, believe that the result of the election in 1920 must be observed and the new frontier established by it respected. The Danes seem to realize the necessity of living in peace with their German neighbors and they desire that the national differences may not be hateful struggles but peaceful competitions and an exchange of culture marked by mutual respect and understanding.

The price to be paid for this kind of relation will doubtless be dear. It will call for an accommodation of differences. But above all else it will demand a just, fair, and liberal treatment of the national minorities on each side of the new frontier. But it seems strange that already so many of the German people probably are completely ignorant, as are perhaps most other peoples, of this seemingly small but in reality rather large question in the north of Germany. This condition involves great danger to Denmark. Many German politicians of the conservative factions protest against the result of the plebiscite in Slesvig and ask for a revision of the frontier. Some would remove it much further to the north. It is not at all inconceivable that the time may come, as, for instance, it did arrive at the beginning of the World War, when the whole German people may be seized by a wild natural enthusiasm. Then the pan-Germans or "Jingoists" may be able to convince the voters that a large German population wants to be delivered from Danish domination and tyranny! Just this is likely to happen if the agreement of the Treaty of Versailles is not rigidly observed and if the rights of each national minority are not fully and mutually respected. And already a difference in the treatment of these minorities has appeared in the matter of providing schools.

These are in brief some facts connected with the tragic events in this part of the history of Denmark which have saddened so many Danish souls and about which the world knows too little. The national sorrows of this country occupy a disproportionate space on the stage of northern Europe. The robbery by Germany in 1864 is an intimate and personal matter with most Danes, some of whom fear that Germany will try to rob again if there is not adequate protection afforded. No sooner had the German heel been lifted, by the benevolence of the Treaty of Versailles, from the stained soil of Slesvig, than painters and poets began to record the nation's joy at the right of that wounded region to return, as an injured and weeping child, to the tender arms of her mother, where she should ever remain. There she shall remain if international honor lives to prevent vaulting ambition from tearing her away again by its unyielding hand of force.

CHAPTER X

Education and National Minorities

IT HAS been noted that education in Slesvig, that part of south Jutland which was restored to Denmark, the mother country, in 1920, is in reality a larger national problem than at first appears. It was also noted that although it seems small it is, nevertheless, a question which should interest other peoples inasmuch as in it is involved the troublesome question of the treatment of national minorities. The manner by which Denmark is solving the educational part of the problem should now be pointed out.

Even during the preparations for the plebiscite, provided under the Treaty of Versailles and already noted, it became quite obvious that if the frontier between Denmark and Germany should as a result of the election be moved farther to the south, there would be many people who, although becoming Danish in a political sense, would remain German in a national sense. When the matter of the proposed election came up at the peace conference at Versailles in March following the armistice, Denmark maintained that special guarantees by means of treaties were not necessary. She believed that sufficient guarantees were offered in the liberal Danish legislation which would apply to all Danish subjects in Slesvig, without regard to language and national feelings. In this legislation which was already in force, freedom as to education and the maintenance and the free use of the language of the minorities was an important and guiding principle.

Education and National Minorities 105

The basis of this legislation was constitutional. It related to the freedom of Danish subjects and allowed full liberty as to education. It gave also full religious liberty, freedom of the press, the right of association and of assembly, and secured the inviolability of the home and of property against arbitrary treatment by the executive power. Moreover, a system of proportional representation, which is in general use for public elections in Denmark, gives any minority, whether political or national, the widest possible opportunity to obtain a just and equitable representation. The general laws of Denmark contain no exceptions by which subjects who belong to a minority are deprived of any rights which other Danish subjects enjoy. Danish law views all Danish subjects as equal, with the same civic and political rights and privileges, regardless of national feelings,—a very liberal as well as just and necessary view.

At the peace conference the Danish position on this point was accepted. No provision was made in the Treaty of Versailles, so far as Denmark was concerned, for the protection of the rights of that German minority which became Danish subjects as a result of the plebiscite in February, 1920, when the frontier between the two countries was moved further to the south. Nor did the Danish cosignatories consider it necessary to include such provisions in the treaty concluded in July of that year between Denmark, and Great Britain, France, Italy, and Japan, in regard to the transfer of sovereignty over that part of Slesvig which returned by vote to Denmark. Germany later expressed the desire for a Danish-German treaty dealing with the subject of the

Danish minority south and the German minority north of the frontier. But Denmark saw diplomatic difficulties in the proposal. Moreover, Denmark maintained that the best basis for peaceful and safe conditions satisfactory to each minority concerned was not to be found in or established by treaties. Such a basis lay, she held, rather in the will of each nation to provide and to maintain and guarantee a legal position satisfactory and just to each minority. All political parties in Denmark, including the conservatives and the labor party, endorsed this point of view.

It is, therefore, rather important to remember that Denmark's present policy in dealing with the German minority in north Slesvig is not required by treaty. It is a voluntary policy. It is the result of Denmark's own sense of fairness and justice to that national minority which now happens to be Danish subjects. It is a policy adopted on Denmark's own initiative. This German minority is perhaps one-fourth of the population in that territory reunited with Denmark. But it should be noted in this connection that almost all of that minority is of the same race as the other people of Jutland. Most of them understand Danish and use it in their homes. Danish is their native language. Moreover, they profess, as do almost all Danes,—almost all the Danish people are confirmed members of the state church—the Evangelical-Lutheran faith. The German-mindedness of this minority is due to peculiar historical developments of Slesvig rather than to German descent or to an original German language in south Jutland. Inasmuch, then, as this minority does not differ in race or religion from the people among whom it lives, the Danish policy in dealing with it has had to concern itself largely with the matters of language and schools. The legal relations on those subjects should now be noted.

In the towns of North Slesvig the elementary schools are divided into two sections. In one of these sections Danish is the language of instruction. In the other section German is the language used. Parents and guardians of children have the right to choose between the two sections. Those children attending the section using Danish as the language of instruction have the opportunity of four to six lessons in German weekly, after the third school year. Those children who attend the section which uses German as the language of instruction have the privilege of the same number of lessons in Danish weekly after the same school year. But this language instruction is not obligatory on the parents and guardians who may have their children exempted from it, and the time thus saved may be used in other school subjects. In the country communities and smaller boroughs the language of instruction in the schools depends upon the language of the people in the school district. If it is Danish, the instruction is in Danish. If it is German, the work of the school is conducted in that language. Could any arrangement be fairer or wiser?

If the language of instruction is Danish, the people must vote on the desirability of a special course with German as the basis of instruction if ten per cent of the voters of the school district having parental authority over children of school age express this desire to the local school board. If such an election is called, and if twenty per cent of the qualified voters having parental authority over children of school age vote for German as the language of instruction, such a course must be provided for those who desire it. If less than twenty per cent of the voters desire this course, it must still be provided, if such voters represent as many as twenty-four children of legal school age. Full provision therefore is made to protect the rights and meet the needs of the minority in every school community.

These are the general regulations which form the basis of school management in that part of Slesvig which was returned to Denmark under the provisions of the Treaty of Versailles. According to the latest reports there are about thirty elementary schools or school sections in that community in which about 3000 children receive instruction in the German language. At the same time about 22,000 pupils were reported in elementary schools which used Danish as the basis of instruction. Of course instruction in Danish is given in those schools or school sections which have German as the basis of instruction; and instruction in German is given in those which have Danish as the basis of instruction, wherever there is a real desire among a sufficiently large minority. In most cases the instruction in the minor language is about four to six lessons a week, as pointed out above, though in others the number has reached twelve and in one case fifteen lessons a week. About 900 weekly lessons in German are given in the elementary schools or school sections which have Danish as the basis of instruction.

In the towns also the Danish ministry of education has established what is known as middle school classes—the school years from eleven to fifteen, a sort of junior high school plan—with

German as the basis of instruction. These classes are set up in connection with municipal schools. They are supported by the Danish state government just as the municipal elementary schools are supported. These educational rights of the German minority in Slesvig are in no way dependent for protection upon the local school authorities. They are all protected by the higher educational authorities of the kingdom, including the state ministry of education. Local school boards also include minority representation which may record its opinion and have it submitted to the ministry. And the ministry of education has given careful consideration to all minority opinions which have come to it on matters relating to schools in Slesvig. Dissatisfaction or complaints with the decision of the ministry are unknown, it is reported.

The expenses of the schools in Slesvig are provided under the same laws and rules which apply to the subject in all public schools in Denmark. Even the extra expense in cases of schools divided into Danish and German sections is taken care of under the general law of the land. The Danish state government has also given considerable building grants to those communities which required additional school buildings on account of the divided schools. The ministry of education reports that it has approved every application for such building grants, which involved, together with the increased salaries of teachers, rather large sums.

This liberal educational policy of the Danish government toward the German minority renders less necessary the establishment of German private schools in Slesvig, though the minority may establish them. The regulations of the general Danish school legislation in the matter of compulsory school attendance of children between seven and fourteen years of age apply. The children are exempted from instruction in public elementary schools if their parents or guardians arrange for them instruction not inferior to that generally demanded in such schools. This law applies to all of Denmark, including that part of Slesvig returned in 1920. The supervision of the private education of children of legal school age is in the hands of the local school committee. Only seven private schools with about 330 children have been established. Private schools in Slesvig, of course, as in other parts of Denmark are entitled to receive state aid when they comply with the general requirements on the subject. These requirements are liberal. Before a private elementary school can receive state aid it must provide instruction which in the opinion of the local school committee is at least as good as that given in the public elementary schools. It must have as many as ten pupils. It must not have a greater number of pupils to be taught by one teacher than that fixed for teachers in public elementary schools. Full reports must be furnished the public authorities by those in charge of the school. Its work must be confined to elementary subjects and it must not undertake to do work generally done in other types of schools. It must of course submit to public supervision.

Higher education at public expense was also provided in the larger towns in Slesvig, in accordance with special legislation of 1920. Instruction was in Danish but special classes were established to enable older pupils to finish their schooling with German as the language of instruction.

The problem in regard to the church has been quite similar to that of schools. It has already been mentioned that the German minority belongs to the same religious faith as that of the other people in Slesvig. So here the problem is also one of language. Due regard is given by the ministry of churches to the desires of the minority whose services are conducted in their own language. In all parishes, including those in which church services in the German language are not established, opportunity is given all members of the congregations to receive ministrations in that language. German services are held in more than one-fourth of the churches. In the larger towns two rectors of equal rank may be appointed, one for the Danish and one for the German congregation in the community, each rector using his own language. Besides these special arrangements the general ecclesiastical legislation of Denmark applies. All laws and decrees of the Danish national church which are or may come into force apply to all the Evangelical-Lutheran parishes in Slesvig as elsewhere in the kingdom. The people are placed therefore on the same footing as those in other parts of Denmark in all church matters. They are not obliged exclusively to avail themselves of the services of the parochial rector. Free parishes there as in other parts of Denmark may use the national churches for services, may have another rector appointed, and the like. The Danish state church is liberal in its doctrine and in its practice as well.

The rights of the German minority are as fully protected in legal procedure as in school and church interests. Written or verbal addresses by the parties to a suit or by their attorneys may be given in German. If necessary the proceedings shall be conducted with the aid of an interpreter retained by the court and paid for out of public funds. The same practice is followed in regard to the translation of legal documents submitted in such cases. All writs or other processes by which the court exercises its jurisdiction, when served in the German language, must be accompanied by a Danish translation, the cost of which is also a legitimate public charge. The judges generally speak German and most of the permanent residents speak Danish, so these rules have not been often applied.

While the Danish government follows this policy with regard to the German minority—all political parties in Denmark being united on it—the various German parties apparently have been unable until quite recently to agree on a policy of treatment for the Danish minority in south Slesvig. That minority is quite large. Only one Danish elementary school in the northern part of the city of Flensborg has been established and none in the southern part of the city, except a divided school. There is not a single Danish school in the country districts though the Danish minority there has often asked for Danish schools. There is one Danish private school in Flensborg, but it is supported by the Danish and not the German government. There is not a single church in which services may be held in Danish. This difference in policy has been disturbing many Danes, some of whom believe the difficulties in Slesvig are not yet settled. Some even are open in their prophecies of another war with Germany which may be even more disastrous than that of

1864 unless the strong arms of neighbors and friends should be extended in protection. In this strength the Danes have hope.

Just recently, however, the Prussian government has announced the grant of what was described in the press as "far-reaching concessions" in the sphere of education to the Danish minority in the frontier districts of Slesvig. Under the regulations now issued local educational authorities are bound to "recognize the need for the establishment" of a state elementary school adapted to the requirements of the Danish minority, upon the application of the parents or guardians of as many as twenty-four children who are subject to the school attendance law. These conditions and regulations are practically identical with those which the Danish government established to meet the needs of the German minorities, immediately after the frontier between the two countries was moved farther to the south. Private schools for the Danish minority in south Slesvig are recognized and subsidies are granted by the German government in the same manner and under the same conditions as such schools for the German minority in north Slesvig are recognized and aided by the Danish government, if application is made on behalf of ten children.

In the German state "minority schools" all instruction is to be given in Danish although the German language is, of course, to be a compulsory subject. The inclusion in the curriculum of the study of Danish history, national customs, and the like is allowed. In the approved private "minority schools" teachers may be employed who have received their training in Denmark; and the parents or their committees may be consulted upon the appointment of teachers in the state minority schools. The Danish community may establish private schools of a type more advanced than the elementary schools and subsidies may be granted to them in the same way as they are granted to German private schools of similar type. Only those persons are considered as belonging to the Danish minority who were born or whose parents were born in the frontier community or in Denmark.

In dealing with the question of the education of the Danish minority in Slesvig, Germany adopted, exactly six years after the plebiscite called for under the Treaty of Versailles, a policy which closely resembles that which Denmark has been following in dealing with German minorities in Slesvig since the plebiscite. The recent announcement of Germany, in view of the controversy with Signor Mussolini over the treatment of the German-speaking minorities in south Tyrol, is hailed with some pride in Berlin as an example of the way Germany treats national minorities within her borders. It seems quite a pity, however, that the announcement in the case of Slesvig which has presented a problem for six years should have followed the controversy in Tyrol, the prominence of which doubtless hastened the decision to make concessions in Slesvig and perhaps favorably affected the extent of it. The years just ahead will tell whether in practice the policy of Germany in Slesvig will prove as extensive and liberal as it now appears and sounds. If Germany desires to treat national minorities within her borders as she would have her own treated in other countries, attention will presumably be turned next to the Polish minority in Germany, which of course will not be a very popular task.

CHAPTER XI

Training Elementary Teachers

THE minister of education or superintendent of schools in Denmark is a woman and her name is Mrs. Nina Bang. She says the plan in use in her country for training teachers for the common schools is antique.

It would not be safe to assume the interest of many American readers in the administrative organization of the Danish school system. With the exception of a few specialists in school administration who probably already know about it, the subject would not engage the attention of a great many people. The simplicity of educational organization and of educational machinery is interesting, however, to one viewing it on the spot and comparing it with the complex systems which prevail in some American states. Moreover, the little educational machinery of the Danes is not allowed to mechanize the spirit of teaching and of learning. Denmark has enacted few school laws since the outline of the present system was established more than one hundred years ago, and the last general act was passed in 1903.

In being content with a minimum of laws Denmark has escaped the confusion which many American communities encounter. For the last three or four years, however, a rather able school commission has been sitting and its work and proposed reforms seem promising. But the Danes seem to have known all along just what they wanted to do in the schools and how it could be done, and they framed a few pieces of intelligent legislation and on these have done a great deal of educating. They are not afflicted with a madness for legislating which is one of the curses of the United States. A rather keenly observing Danish woman has just returned after several years in America and has been publishing in the newspapers in her country some articles on American conditions as she viewed them. One of the conditions which she does not understand is the large number of seemingly trivial and senseless laws which each legislature enacts. She poked fun at this tendency and practice, in the good-natured Danish way, but concluded that it was a mania of mediocrities who somehow find their way into law-making bodies and in order to make their names temporarily secure in the minds of their constituencies succeed in getting such laws passed. This seemed a rather rough conclusion, but even an American must admit that she did not miss the point altogether.

Just now, however, the socialists in Denmark would revise the school laws, but they are not yet strong enough. They have plans for revision as soon as their strength is sufficient. Wilhelm Rasmussen, a socialist member of the present parliament, yesterday laid them out on a piece of paper, over a cup of tea, in his office at the High School for Teachers, of which he is also principal. And Mrs. Nina Bang, the minister of education, who appointed him to this position, is eager for certain changes.

She was one of the first people the North Carolinian interviewed. She is a very kindly disposed woman, at least to visitors, but, among the school workers of Denmark and some other people also, she is apparently very unpopular. She is not a professional educator, but more of a professional politician, and she owes her present position to the success of the socialists in the last election. "What was the occupation of the prime minister before he was elevated to that rank?" a Copenhagen business man was asked. "A cigar maker," he replied, and holding up a Danish cigar he added: "He made these things." This is a condition which somewhat annoys the Danes, or many of them, and most of the school workers in Denmark are irritated by the fact that this cigar-maker appointed or dictated the appointment of Nina Bang to the ministry of education. They do not like it. There still remains in this country a rather large conservative following.

"What do you think of Mrs. Nina Bang?" a manager of a cigar store was asked, in a town near the capital. He shrugged his shoulders. "In Denmark we say 'No woman at the top.' She is our first woman minister. We hope she is to be our last. It's awful. A gentleman from America comes to Denmark to see our schools. Naturally he wants to see the minister of education. Perhaps," and there was a twinkle in his eye, "perhaps, coming from America, he expects that the minister will serve a drink and that they will smoke cigars. He goes to the office to see the minister. 'Hell, it's a woman,' exclaims the American. I tell you it is no good, no good." The man spoke with feeling about the matter.

The people, or many of them at any rate, do not like Mrs. Bang's dislike of the king, because the Danes generally love their king. He is a plain and unassuming man and in high favor with the people. At the Royal Theatre recently the orchestra played the national anthem. Mrs.

Bang was present and so was King Christian the Tenth. The people stood, all except Mrs. Bang, who remained seated quite sullenly because the song praised the king. In some of the theatres she is often the subject of burlesque, but so are other officials and prominent people. The Danish wit and wag does not spare anybody. The funny papers and magazines caricature her continuously. One criticism of her is that since she became minister of education she has taken a fancy to dismissing or trying to dismiss people she did not personally or politically like. One paper a few days ago showed her on her holiday at a bathing beach somewhere in southern Europe. She was talking excitedly to an attendant or life-saver, and the legend read: "You are dismissed from the first of the month." Among those she has tried to dismiss is a very lovable and apparently quite capable school inspector. She rang and he appeared in her office. "You are dismissed," said Mrs. Bang. "Very well," said the inspector. But in a moment he returned and said: "You can't do that. The king appointed me." So he had and so she couldn't. That seems to have closed the incident officially, but the newspapers learned of it and made much fun. As minister of education in Denmark Mrs. Nina Bang seems not to be giving strength to the idea that women can successfully administer large public affairs. She is rather deepening the doubt in Denmark of their ability to do it.

She sat across the table in one of those elegant conference rooms of the beautiful Danish parliament house, answering some questions which her subordinates, inspectors, assistants, and clerks had uniformly but courteously declined to answer.

Their answer would always be: "Will you please speak with the minister on that point. She has her own ideas and is just now preparing something for the Parliament." One of the questions concerned the plan for training teachers for the folk schools (the elementary or common schools), into which some excellent features had been read by the North Carolinian who wanted to know what the minister thought of it.

It was the opening week of the Parliament and Mrs. Bang appeared somewhat tired. She had been busy. She begged to change the appointment from one to two o'clock in the afternoon. The minister of finance was to make an important report at one. She was very sorry to make such a request but she would return at two. Could she be excused? It seemed a reasonable request and she was allowed to go to hear another member of the cabinet tell how many million kroner would be required by the kingdom to administer during the coming fiscal period such things as schools, justice, poor relief, unemployment, old age pensions, the interest on the national debt, and the royal household expenses, and to tell also where he thought the kroner would be found. So the visitor found himself agreeable to her request and Mrs. Nina Bang was allowed to learn how the money was to be raised to pay her wages of eighteen thousand kroner a year. When she returned she was asked: "What do you think of the Danish plan for training teachers for the folk schools?" "Antique," she answered.

Now it is perfectly natural that errors consequent upon the misunderstanding of words may creep into one's impressions of things seen and heard in a strange country, where it is necessary for an American to depend upon his own slim knowledge of the language or perhaps upon interpretation and translation. There is also the fact of different standards of money, of weights, of measures, of temperatures, and distances, and the like, even of school work itself, which must be rendered as nearly as possible into equivalent English. This is not always easily done, rarely ever is it safely done, and thus the doors for many mistakes are opened. To describe any feature of the Danish school system so as to make it clear to any readers in the United States who are unfamiliar with it, is for these and other reasons quite difficult. But a word should be said here on the plan for training the teachers of the elementary schools, which the minister of education says is antique. These schools, folk schools, as they are called, are the public elementary schools in which children from seven to fourteen years of age receive such instruction as the law makes obligatory for every child. In them are taught Danish, reading, writing, arithmetic, history, geography, music, natural science, natural history, hygiene, sloyd, and gymnastics.

The training of the teachers in these schools takes place in about eighteen teachers' colleges, some for men, some for women, and some for both men and women. Some of the schools are private but all are supported by public appropriations. The course is three years in length. The candidate for admission must be at least eighteen years of age and must present the appropriate certificates of health, character, vaccination, and the like, show how his time has been spent since leaving the common schools, pass a satisfactory examination on the subjects taught in those schools, demonstrate a knowledge of music and the ability to play simple compositions, and give proof of a year's practice teaching. This must have been under the direction of an able teacher who must certify to the school authorities the candidate's desire and adaptability for the teaching profession. This preliminary practice teaching may be done in the public schools, in private schools with approved teachers, or in one of the model schools attached to the teachers' colleges, where the candidate may also prepare for the examination for admission to these colleges. Completion of the work of the common schools is presupposed, and most of the candidates have had instruction in the folk high schools and other continuation schools, some have been students in the gymnasiums, and some have attended the university.

The course of study in these teachers' colleges includes first of all instruction in the subjects taught in the common schools. These disciplines are rather thorough. Much attention is given also to physical education and music. There is instruction in pedagogy and much practice teaching under competent direction. The practice school may be a local public school or one established especially to serve the teachers' college. The work in pedagogy begins with instruction in elementary psychology, and in the last year the students get five hours a week for at least forty weeks in the general history of education, comparative education, methods, history of education in Denmark, and the organization and administration of the Danish elementary schools, as they have evolved and are now operated.

The satisfactory completion of the work of the teachers' colleges is attested by the results of both oral and written examinations. The oral examination of teachers in Denmark is regarded as very valuable. It provides revelations that written examinations can never make. The certificate granted upon the completion of all the requirements of the teachers' college permits the holder to teach in any public elementary school, but it does not guarantee appointment to a position. The supply of teachers is greater than the demand in Denmark, because of the high regard in which teaching and teachers are held by the public, and because the salaries of teachers are good, and because also there is an excellent plan for pensioning teachers in old age. Positions are filled by orderly procedure and the candidate with the best record gets the vacancy. Good salaries, permanent tenure, and pensions make the profession attractive to rather high grade men and women.

Further training of elementary teachers in service is provided in a rather unique Danish institution about which there is almost nothing published in English. This institution is known as the High School for Teachers and it was founded near the middle of the last century. The school is in Copenhagen. Instruction is free and in addition scholarships with stipends ranging in value from $100 for unmarried to $200 for married people are available for most of the students who come from rural communities. There is also an allowance for books. This is a teachers' college with advanced instruction in the subjects taught in or related to the curriculum of the elementary school. In addition to instruction in these subjects courses are given in phonetics, the history of linguistic development, history of religion, of art, of literature, sociology, economics, and library administration. The school has an excellent staff of special teachers who are drawn from the best teachers in the schools in and around Copenhagen. For the most part they are professors in the university and the technical high schools.

The course in the High School for Teachers extends through a year, and the principle of teaching is strictly scientific. The best qualified candidates are admitted upon examination. Last year more than 200 people applied and only 150 were selected, on an average grade of "very good." This year 207 people were selected from 300 who applied, and upon an average mark of "rather good." The principal of the school now believes that no teacher who is willing to sacrifice time and expense in extending his education should be denied admission; and he frankly says that the less well qualified ones are those who are most in need of the instruction. It is now his purpose to give practically all the younger graduates of the teachers' colleges the opportunity for another year's work at his institution. Home study courses and holiday or summer classes are also provided. Plans are now made also for instruction by radio, so that students of foreign languages may listen to London, Berlin, and Paris, and that some of the lectures of the professors may be broadcasted to the teachers in the rural communities. In the excellent schools of Copenhagen and vicinity opportunity is afforded the students for much observation of teaching. Attendance upon this school is purely voluntary. Professional interest is the only incentive which brings so many applicants every year although it should be noted that the opportunity of a year in Copenhagen is very attractive to the rural teachers. Many of these have already reached their maximum in status and salary, however, (attendance upon the school does not carry with it an increase in salary) but they seem eager to learn more and to improve themselves professionally. There is no examination at the end of the course, but the principal issues to each student a certificate based upon the judgments of the professors.

It is difficult not to indulge in a comparison which may be unpleasant if not very odious. If Mrs. Nina Bang thinks the Danish plan for training teachers for the elementary schools is antique, what would she call the plan in some of the American states, especially the Southern states? Consider the multitudes of little, lifeless, hopelessly uninspiring people, who, in many rural communities of the United States, legally take charge every year of groups of children. With poor academic equipment and still poorer professional training, they often have no teaching experience whatever. Then look closely at the so-called professional training for teachers, especially that pretended in the summer schools, large and small, with their glaring neglect of systematic and thorough instruction in the subject matter of the elementary school, the pompous courses in "education," the so-called "normal" courses, often so misdirected as to shade easily into abnormal courses. It seems positively wrong. It is wrong for those who are too often enticed not by the desire of genuine professional advancement but by required attendance at a short term summer school and the driblet salary increase which such attendance brings. It is wrong also for the children these people must teach. It is sad because so many of the states lack real, systematic plans for the training of elementary school teachers, and sadder because they have not yet been able to gain a real statesman-like view of the great responsibility. Perhaps one of the largest economic wastes in American education is due to the haphazard and planless effort of so many states in the training of teachers.

The teachers in the Danish teachers' colleges are recruited from the ranks of those most successful and experienced in the elementary schools and who have had the best advanced training. They are all rather carefully selected. All of them are apparently quite capable teachers, though probably not all would be so engaging as one whom the visitor delighted to observe.

He was of doubtful age, perhaps fifty-five. He was erect, graceful, and made a curiously statuesque appearance in the class room and hall. His head was large and thatched with silvery hair, and the finely and firmly carved features of his face beneath increased the sculpturesque impression. His clothes were somewhat baggy and his cravat had loosened from his collar, but he did not look slovenly. His eyes were extraordinary, violet-blue, and his mouth was flexible and full of changing expression. His gestures were of dignity and ease and over his face moved an occasional smile of great naturalness. His air, like that of most mature Danes, was one of deep and chastened melancholy. But the aspect of profound sadness which he seemed to maintain so steadily was deceptive, for he had an apostolic, evangelical cheerfulness. Occasionally the aspect of sadness would change to momentary, fleeting humor which delighted his already captivated students, as he revolved some thought involving perhaps some pedagogical inexactitude.

He must have personal popularity as a teacher. A full dozen substantial books declare also his disciplined scholarship which he has humanized in class and out for the well-being of Denmark and her children, whom he loves so passionately. He holds the highest academic degree within the gift of his great university, and it stands for solid learning. All about him was a hospitable kindness which draws men to him instantly and makes them revere him and the profession which he represents. Of his gifts a foreigner could have a taste. Not a hundred consecutive words of the lecture could he understand in that small, only fairly well equipped lecture room. Though his ear was unable to follow intelligently he was witness to the fervid and dignified manner, to the rise and fall of the professor's sonorous periods, and to the rapt attention which he commanded from the class. The impression on the pupils and the visitor was profound and unmistakable. At the beginning of the hour they had participated in a lively discussion, but during the lecture they took never a note. Instead they drank in all that the master said and were visibly moved by his earnestness and by their own sense of responsibility. This Danish teacher of elementary teachers would have made no more stately a figure had he been in full Lutheran canonicals, with the strange frilled ruff about his neck, and a long black robe falling from his shoulders to his feet. As nearly as possible it is this kind of teacher Denmark chooses to prepare those who teach her children.

CHAPTER XII
Training High School Teachers

THE nearly three hundred high schools in little Denmark would interest educational workers almost anywhere, and the plan for training the teachers of these schools and for supervising their work afterwards would doubtless fill the inspector of high schools in almost any American state with pure envy. These schools are perhaps the strongest, the best organized and directed, and the most capably taught of all the Danish educational units. They are carefully supervised by an adequate staff of the best trained and most competent people engaged in education in the entire kingdom. And the preparation of the teachers for these schools is much longer and perhaps much better than that of the teachers for the elementary schools, the plan of which was noted in the preceding chapter.

Dr. Henrik Bertelsen, the inspector of the gymnasium schools (the senior high schools) which prepare for the university and the other higher educational institutions, is counted among the most capable and distinguished educators of Denmark. He is unassuming and modest, though a man of impressive bearing, and instantly he fills a visitor with confidence in his high abilities as an educational leader and with respect for his statesmanlike comprehension of his task. He knows the Danish school system from top to bottom and all of its problems of the present and of the immediate future, and he showed remarkable familiarity with school systems in other countries, particularly

England and the United States. In either of these countries he could easily be taken, not for a professional pedagogue, but for an executive engaged in the direction of a large commercial business. He looks the part of a leader. Perhaps nowhere in Denmark is it likely that one could meet a man of more reassuring dignity and courtesy, or of broader scholarship and learning, qualities and accomplishments which combine to give constant inspiration to the army of secondary teachers whose training he has helped personally to direct and supervise and whose work in the classroom he knows with quite remarkable thoroughness.

His department is large and his official powers are wide. He receives his appointment from the king and does not have to worry about his tenure of office so long as he behaves himself and does his work effectively and well. Nor does he have to consider the fortunes or misfortunes of contesting party politics. He is trained for a high order of service to his country and is free to give professional and undivided attention to the problems of his work. He does not have to stop to consider whether his policies are agreeable to the party which happens to dominate in the government. If they are educationally sound, that is sufficient to enlist the sympathy and support of the people who, while differing perhaps in political views, are united in their confidence in education and expert professional leadership in it. These are views which most American states must gain, for many of them have not yet done so, if justice to all the American youth ever prevails. They must learn the simple educational lesson that each generation, without regard to the religious or political views

A State Normal School

prevailing at the time, is in duty bound to serve as trustee for posterity, that the state owes to her youth of today the best that can be given, and that she can go forward only on the feet of her children.

In an ancient building of frigid and somewhat forbidding exterior,—as is the appearance of so many public offices in Europe,—in Frederiksholms Kanal in Copenhagen, Dr. Bertelsen sat at his desk in an office as clean as a pin and entirely free from the litter and the feverishness of educational administration, the noise of typewriters and adding machines, and the chatter of typists and clerks. The place was serene. The inspector was induced to talk of his department, of his tasks and duties and policies, and through it all he revealed a reliable professional pride which excited the admiration of his visitor, who was led to see how easily a government can have wise and definite, obtainable objectives for its schools and for the training of its teachers. But he was also led to see that such a program can be set up and carried forward by a people only through proper leadership. Never yet has it been achieved by policies of timid opportunism and expediency.

The pupils who enter the beginning class in a Danish senior high school (gymnasium) which has a three years' course have all had a thorough elementary education of five years and in addition a thorough secondary education (junior high school) of four years. The teachers in the senior high schools must therefore be able to give a still more advanced secondary training. Preparation to give this calls for a long and rather severe training in the University of Copenhagen where all such teachers are prepared in academic, professional, and practical courses which extend over a period of about six or seven years.

There are three courses in the typical Danish gymnasium or senior high school, the classical course, the modern language course, and the scientific course, with certain subjects such as Danish, French, history, natural history, physical education, and music common to all courses. The program is rather flexible. All the schools are controlled and in part supported by the central government. Graduation carries with it the privilege of admission to the university and to the other colleges of the kingdom, but these institutions have nothing to do with the final gymnasium examinations which are controlled by the department of education under the direction of the inspector of the gymnasium schools.

The graduate of one of these schools who desires to enter the work of teaching in a gymnasium matriculates in the university. During the first year he pursues somewhat general studies, somewhat in the nature of the orientation courses which some American colleges have recently set up for the freshmen. This course with a compulsory examination (which is generally oral) at the end of the year is required of all students in all faculties in the university. Rector Torm explained last fall that it had become necessary years ago when the senior high schools were not so thorough as now and that it had been continued because it had been found very useful. In time, however, it might be abandoned, he thought. As the work of the gymnasium schools strengthened, the need for the course would obviously become less and less urgent.

With this general course many freshmen may and often do begin also their program for the remainder of their university work. This may be in the faculty of arts (letters) or in the faculty of science. Both are rather comprehensive departments of university work and afford the student opportunity to continue courses which engaged his interest in the gymnasium, to which he now plans to return as a teacher. Whether his interest is in science or arts this prospective gymnasium teacher selects a major and a minor subject and he is at liberty, within certain restrictions, to combine any of the subjects which are taught in the gymnasium. But his training is in definite preparation to teach a definite subject in that school and to teach it well. The training and the demands of the examination in his major and minor studies are definite, thorough, and rigid. These facts contain for educational leaders in most American states quite obvious lessons. They would, however, likely answer: "But how can we do it?" and their answer would reveal another one of the educational weaknesses of too many of the states, the lack of imagination and of energy.

If this candidate for a place to teach in a Danish gymnasium selected, let us say, English as his major subject, he must not only be thorough in the English work done in the gymnasium but he must also be able to use English, orally as well as written (which American high school teachers of modern foreign languages are rarely trained to do); and he must have a thorough theoretical knowledge of the grammar and phonetics and of the development of the language, acquired through a study of Anglo-Saxon and Middle English. He must also have a knowledge of English literature and of modern English social institutions and know something of critical philological methods. The required reading representing English and American literature extends from Alfred to Bernard Shaw, and on this the candidate does many papers and is subjected to many oral examinations by his professors. In addition he must make a special study on which he will generally be required to do a lengthy thesis. If English is his minor subject less work will of course be required and stress will be laid on modern language and literature. The same or similar demands are made for the other modern foreign languages. If history is the major subject a solid knowledge of historical developments from ancient to modern times becomes the basis for a careful study of certain particular periods, to which is added a study of national economy and of constitutional law, and also training in the use of historical sources.

If this candidate wishes to become a teacher of mathematics or science in the high school, he chooses between the mathematical-scientific (mathematics, physics, chemistry, astronomy) and the natural history (zoölogy, botany, geology, geography, physiology) groups, and the courses he pursues are based upon work which he did in the gymnasium. If he chooses the first group his work in the university will fall into three divisions each of which terminates with an examination. In the first division he gets a broad and solid basis in mathematics, chemistry, physics, and astronomy. This work is followed by that of a more pedagogical nature and the textbooks in use in the gymnasiums in these subjects are carefully studied and treated from a scientific and didactic point of view. Proficiency in making school experiments in chemistry and physics is developed and in addition the history of science is studied. Then a particular domain of science is subjected to a detailed study in which theses are prepared.

Much the same procedure is followed if the student has chosen the natural history group of zoölogy, botany, and the like. In this group, however, he must attend a course in chemistry during the first year, and if his work in the gymnasium should have been largely in languages and social subjects, he must also attend a course in physics. Then follows a long and serious study of zoölogy and botany, histology, botanical anatomy, physics, geology and geography, and physiology, with much experimental work and excursions. All this work of training gymnasium teachers in Denmark is carefully and definitely planned. The completion of it in whatever faculty gives the degree of master of arts, a degree, however, which is superior to the equivalent degree in the United States, and in many cases it represents as much or even more solid work than that of the doctor's degree in many institutions in this country.

Now this candidate to teach in a Danish gymnasium must attend a practical course at a gymnasium and in addition a theoretical course at the university. This latter course includes pedagogy, school hygiene and school management, the history of education, school law, the history of school reforms and theories, and physical education, and extends over about a year. During this time the practical course (a course in practice teaching) at a gymnasium may also be followed. Generally, therefore, the student gets his practice teaching in a gymnasium in or near Copenhagen. This work is conducted by experienced gymnasium teachers who are selected by the inspector of the gymnasium schools. The candidate attends seven lessons a week in his major and five lessons in his minor subject, the teaching being done, after a short time, alternately by himself and the regular teachers. This practical course concludes in a test or examination of some lessons given by the candidate in his major and minor subjects in the presence of the teacher, the principal of the school, and the inspector of the gymnasium schools or some representative sent by him.

The ability of the candidate as a practical teacher of gymnasium work is expressed in a mark by this committee. Three marks are given: "passed;" "passed well;" and "passed excellently." The candidate must get the mark of "passed well" in order to be recommended for a post in a gymnasium. To the certificate bearing this mark and signed by the inspector is added a testimony of the teachers, under whom the practice teaching was done, and of the principal.

These certificates and testimonies are not forms to be filled in and signed. They are individual, and each has character. A set of these papers was found in possession of an excellent "adjunct" (there are three ranks of teachers in the gymnasium: "adjunct," which is the beginning teacher; "lektor," the next rank; and principal) in a Copenhagen gymnasium. He consented to their use here if names and other marks of indentification were deleted. The Danes are very modest. This young man thought it very improper to publish his certificate, even in the United States. The first one, not given here, is a statement that the candidate passed his examination in "practical proficiency of teaching" and that he passed "with high honors," and it is signed by the inspector of the gymnasiums of Denmark who attended his examinations.

The testimony of the teacher under whom he did his practice teaching in his major subject certifies that the candidate passed a certain year in a certain gymnasium, attending instruction in English, and then adds: "He has a particularly good faculty for teaching; he gets into his work thoroughly and energetically and has a pronounced aptitude for it. He has acquired a considerable skill in applying sound methods in his subject. Furthermore, he is able to make good use of his professional knowledge in his teaching, to interest his pupils, and to adapt the material to them, at the same time maintaining discipline by his friendly conduct towards them. We have no doubt of his ability as a skillful teacher." This was signed by the teacher and by the principal of the school.

The teacher of the minor subject (German) in which the candidate received practice in the same school stated: "He has displayed the greatest diligence and interest. His faculty of concentrating and of keeping the attention of his pupils in the upper as well as in the lower classes is considerable, so that he is able to carry out the principles of group instruction with ease and exactness. His firm, yet friendly, appearance, makes him a master of discipline, and his solid knowledge and preparation enable him harmoniously to let all the details of his subject tell to full advantage. We believe he will make a particularly skillful teacher." This was signed by the teacher of the minor subject and by the principal of the school.

Now this young man was ready to apply for a place as "adjunct" in a gymnasium, but he was not guaranteed a post. When he got it, however, which happened to be quite immediately, he received a fair salary, increasing on a sliding scale, which is the same for all high school teachers of equal rank. In due time he will be promoted to "lektor," if he grows professionally, and later he may become principal. In old age he will be pensioned by the government. Throughout his career as teacher he will be held in as high esteem as any other professional group in his country and respected for his knowledge, his thorough training, and his professional skill. He continues his studies in summer or other vacations in England and on the continent, but he pursues his professional interests on his own account. Though not blessed with much of this world's goods this particular young man, who is a good representative of the gymnasium teachers of Denmark, has in his little five-room flat on the top floor of a house in a far from fashionable part of Copenhagen, where he lives with his wife and little daughter, more books than most American college professors accumulate in a life time.

During his teaching experience he will continue to receive professional aid and encouragement from the inspector of gymnasiums and his staff of six assistants. These are high grade teachers from the field. They teach three days a week in their own schools and the other three days they help the gymnasium teachers of their own subjects in other schools. A more beautiful piece of organization cannot be found anywhere than this part of the high school work in Denmark. These helping teachers, as they may be called, are always welcome to the gymnasium teachers who regard the inspector of gymnasiums and his organization as able and helpful.

The Danes, like most Europeans, say to their prospective gymnasium teachers: "Prepare to teach something. Learn much and learn it well. Learn how to teach it and demonstrate the capacity and then we shall permit you to instruct our children." This seems a most sensible demand. To the children it is the only just one. It seems so much more reasonable, a better and a fairer demand, than the practice in many of the American states. There, too general and often poorly related college subjects conducted without professional emphasis, added to a few so-called professional courses, too often constitute the required preparation for high school teaching. Demonstrated ability to teach is not yet sufficiently demanded. The emphasis is too much on so many hours or courses of a professional nature which alone cannot make teachers or much of a contribution to the profession. They are valueless unless they are supported by a solid and wide knowledge of the subject matter to be taught in the schools. The paper credits which periodically, particularly at the close of summer schools, are shipped to state departments of education are a mere gesture in the direction of professional training. They are essentially characterless and quite doubtful evidence of ability to teach, even though they may appear on duplicate or triplicate cards of uniform size, which are indexed, catalogued, cross-referenced, finger-printed, filed, and sometimes, fortunately perhaps, misplaced and lost.

Resources enough there are at hand in the United States for a better and more definite plan for the training of high school teachers. Vision, imagination, and industry could shortly organize, correlate, and make full use of them. The colleges and universities now naturally have the monopoly in this field. But too few if any of them have been willing to face the situation squarely and to organize and equip themselves properly for the task. The records, moreover, show too few of the high school teachers teaching subjects in which they have had definite and adequate academic and professional preparation, and fewer still who have had opportunity for practice teaching under expert guidance before beginning their work. No teacher-training school is worthy the name that is not fully equipped with facilities for observation and practice teaching by the prospective teachers; and a state stands in her own light in failing to require the candidate to demonstrate his fitness and ability to teach before he is allowed a position. Improvement here would not only greatly strengthen the secondary schools of the United States, it would bring inspiration to hosts of high school children, strengthen the work of the colleges, and help mightily to develop in this country a real profession of teaching.

CHAPTER XIII

WINNING HIGHER DEGREES

REFERENCE has been made elsewhere to the universal respect in which education and learning are held by the Danes. This respect is in evidence not only in the urban centers but in the rural communities as well. Solid scholarship, science, substantial technical skill, and cleverness are in high favor almost everywhere in Denmark. The word "clever" is used very much by the people, meaning talent, brightness, quickness of intellect, intellectual adroitness rather than obliging good nature, as it is not uncommonly heard in colloquial usage in the United States. A clever person excites the admiration of the Danes. He is never frowned upon by them, unless he is conspicuous for smartness and pertness. Generally he is approved everywhere he appears.

The respect which the people have for learning and for correct information is seen generally throughout Denmark but especially in Copenhagen. The lectures at the university and at other public places are always largely attended, not only by the so-called academic people but also by many other classes. All university lectures, except a few on purely professional subjects, are open to everybody, even those not entitled to matriculation in the institution, and this privilege is open to any man or woman who has passed the *Studenterexamen*. The Copenhagen papers give much space to the activities of the university, and the columns are closely watched by the people for subjects in which they are interested. Many kinds of people attend the special lectures, not only those who are set on careers of professional scholars, but often tradespeople and workmen are seen there also. The institution is very democratic in its appeal and in its influence.

The large audiences which always witness the examination for the doctorate at the university give substantial evidence of widespread interest in scholarship and learning. This degree is not only much more difficult to obtain in Denmark but it seems generally to be a higher academic distinction than in the United States. It is usually acquired only by those university graduates who follow scholarship or science as a profession and it is awarded after years of study and productive research. Honorary degrees are very rare. They are never given as a sycophantic sop to some political or ecclesiastical Cerberus, as they have been known to be awarded in some instances in American universities. One would probably never hear in Copenhagen such a story as has been told on one American institution. Its president had as his guest the president of another university. They were viewing the campus and its fine buildings. "What did that building cost you?" inquired the visiting president. "Two LL.D. degrees," replied the host.

Now, of course, it may be recalled that "Doctor" Cook caught Copenhagen napping and received honor in the great festival hall of Copenhagen University, but so far as it has been possible to determine, this is the only scandal connected with honorary degrees at the institution. That is after all not so reprehensible, because the world nodded for a time when Cook made his announcement. It is true that the people at the university do not like to talk about the incident, though they are good-natured about it. But the fact was faintly recalled and the files of the newspapers verified it. The university is still humiliated. An enthusiastic alumnus said: "Dr. Cook spoke from that desk," pointing to the rector's stand in the great hall, but he never added, as he could have done: "And we gave him a degree." The guest saved the feelings of his guide who could have been greatly mortified by the frightful reminder. But the alumnus could also have been told that any American university from Harvard down to the smallest provincial college would have stampeded, under the same circumstances, to decorate the artless deceiver.

The average age of those receiving the doctor's degree at Copenhagen is considerably higher than that of those receiving it in American universities. At the *Aarsfest* (commencement) last fall the average age of the twenty-five men promoted to the degree at that time was above thirty-five years. This is in contrast to the youth of many Ph.D.'s in the United States where the manufacture of doctors has sometimes grown to quite an industry. In Denmark the degree does not so much decorate the name of the holder, as he by his learning and scholarship adorns, dignifies, and ennobles the degree. It is never given as it has been given in the United States to callow fledglings, equipped with infantile moustaches, Dunhill pipes, some so-called graduate credits, and an anemic thesis on some narrow, rather lifeless subject. Here the degree has nothing to do with course credit. It is awarded only on the basis of real achievement and as a reward for demonstrated learning of a solid and useful kind. The dissertation is apparently not the end, as it too often is in the United States, but the beginning of productive scholarship. For this reason the degree is highly respected in Denmark. And the examination which in part determines the fitness of the candidate for the degree arouses much interest among people who generally, in the United States at least, would not be expected to have interest in such matters. The large audiences which attend the examinations are also in sharp contrast to the altogether too small committees who conduct the ceremony in American universities where the examination is generally not open to the public. It would be an interesting experiment to open a few to public view and study the attendance.

A hall quite as spacious as Gerrard at the University of North Carolina, capable of accommodating an audience of four or five hundred people, is always packed to overflowing when one of these examinations is held in Copenhagen. Yesterday it was packed a full half hour in advance, when a candidate in medicine was to defend his thesis. This dealt with "A Biological Method of Comparison with the White Corpuscles as a Standard," a technical subject, but practical enough to draw many people to hear it discussed. The morning papers had carried a picture of the candidate and an announcement of the examination and the general subject of the thesis which was to be defended at two o'clock in the afternoon. The candidate had completed the medical course at the university in 1919 and had been admitted to practice after the customary hospital service, a very comprehensive training of fifteen months.

But he was not yet entitled to be called "doctor," but only "candidate (bachelor) in medicine." He had studied in Paris also. Now he offered his researches,—the results of careful experiments which he had conducted at the Institute of Pathology—an elaborately printed book, as the basis of his claim for the coveted degree.

The candidate, in full evening clothes, faced a battery of cameras when he entered the court of the university. All candidates for the degree are so attired, even though the examination is always held in the early afternoon. While the two opponents nominated by the university to attack his thesis were trying to find flaws in it, reporters and artists were writing the story of the contest and sketching the contestants for Danish readers the following morning. That night the leading daily in Denmark flashed on its bulletin board at the city hall square the news: "Candidate in medicine and surgery, Sven Kiaer, today became doctor," along with other domestic and foreign news items of interest to the crowds who throng the streets at night. The following morning all the papers carried photographs and sketches of the candidate and of the opponents in action, and gave to the examination and the scientific significance of the thesis considerable space, almost as much as American dailies give to the sprained ankle of some Virginia or North Carolina football player just before a Thanksgiving game. This examination was not exceptional, although the thesis was considered quite a contribution to medical science.

An examination which also attracted wide notice was that of "Docent" (instructor or tutor) Aage Brusendorff, who shortly afterwards was selected by the faculty of the university to succeed Professor Otto Jespersen, the well-known English scholar, under whom the candidate had studied. One paper the following morning carried over the news story of the examination the headline: "Festive tournament at the university." The lead to the story ran this way: "There was such a run on the university yesterday that one would have thought that it was not an academic act that was going to be performed, but a notorious lawsuit, like the Landsmandsbank affair," a reference to a bank failure which had caused great excitement in Denmark. "The reserved seats were all occupied by distinguished representatives of the learned world," and here followed the names of many old and young professors and instructors and noted men outside the university. "The pit, the balcony, and the gallery were filled with a keenly interested audience of both sexes. This very great interest is easily explained," the paper continued, "by the fact that the candidate does not belong to the usual sort of candidates for the doctorate who disappear from the university as soon as they have won their doctor's degree. But he is on the contrary determined to be wedded to the professor's chair. Another interesting fact is that the chief opponent is the very same professor of whom the candidate is the rumored successor; our own great scholar, Otto Jespersen, who, moreover, was on this occasion acting for the very last time on the arena of our university."

The dean of the philosophical faculty opened the ceremony by giving for the benefit of the audience a summary of the history of the thesis. Originally it was prepared in Danish and accepted by the faculty in 1920. Later on it was rewritten, enlarged and published in English by a publisher of high repute in Europe and the United States. The study dealt with the "Chaucer Tradition."

Professor Jespersen, the first official opponent, began by comparing the irregularities of the genesis of the thesis (on an English subject but submitted in Danish) to the irregularities of the examination: the chief opponent being an ex-teacher. Then the distinguished scholar abandoned himself to a panegyric of Chaucer, his favorite author. "He is a wonderful story-teller," he said, "and he gives an invaluable description of English life in the fourteenth century. His description is also marked by a deep sense of humor." And here the professor took a little dig at another examination, recently held; he said: "The way in which I understand humor is the simple and ordinary one and not such a profound one as has lately been made fashionable within the philosophical faculty, which requires fifty pages to explain what humor is," and there was great laughter in the hall.

Then the official opponent paid a compliment to the candidate for his treatment of the subject. "Your book is not only the largest dissertation on the subject but also the weightiest and the most valuable. It is a work that cannot be neglected. Your learning is enormous. If Carlyle were right in calling him a genius who has the power of taking pains, then you are a genius,—but, by the way, Carlyle is not right." He reproached the candidate for "his disregard of predecessors like Skeat." "Will you allow me to make an observation?" asked the candidate with great authoritativeness: "Skeat has ascribed six poems to Chaucer which he notoriously has not written." To this

Professor Jespersen only answered with a deep ironical emphasis: "Notoriously? Well!" and there was great laughter again.

The candidate's picture of the old verse-copyist and second-hand bookseller, Shirley, was very pleasing to Professor Jespersen, because, among other things, it harmonized exactly with the picture of him that is given in Skeat, whom the candidate otherwise, in his great anxiety to get home on his predecessor, held in such contempt. "The same anxiety also appears," Professor Jespersen went on, "when he tells us that Miss Hammond is such and such. . . ."

Then the candidate darted up with: "I never said so."

"Didn't you?" asked Professor Jespersen rather inexorably. Just look at the note on page 58. As regards your English language, it is fairly good. But you have a favorite word that is not so good. It is 'meaningless' which is used by you not less than seven times and always in the sense of 'absurd,' which it does not mean at all. It means 'having no importance' and that is something quite different. "But," he added, as the candidate bowed his head with a blush, "old Storm was guilty of the same error and he knew English pretty well in other respects. So do not be sorry. You are in good company."

Professor Jespersen ended by praising the candidate for his diligence, learning, and insight. "You have won for yourself a fine place in the line of Chaucer scholars, besides Bradford, Miss Hammond, and—(emphatically) Skeat," and there was tremendous applause. The candidate thanked his master for his very friendly opposition and for all that he had meant to him for so many years. "Professor Jespersen has taught us to subordinate the detail to the broad view," said Mr. Brusendorff.

It was now that the North Carolina visitor was made to feel at home. The next official opponent appeared to be more interested in the details than in the broad view. The visitor could easily fancy himself in his own faculty meeting listening or appearing to listen to some colleague suggest a delicate rearrangement of a sentence in the report of some committee. The opponent went over parts of the thesis comma by comma, but as a rule the candidate answered very well, and often in a language as slighting as if the opponent had been Skeat. Once the candidate admitted with a sort of acid smile that perhaps the opponent was right. "Such an admission," remarked a morning newspaper, "is in academic language formulated thus: 'The theories of the highly honored opponent are, I think, very pleasing,'" When he spat out the word "pleasing" a wave of laughter rolled through the critical and interested audience. But there was nothing to be sorry about, especially for the candidate who throughout the entire examination showed such certitude and elegance as few candidates for the doctorate possess. Shortly afterwards Mr. Brusendorff became Doctor Brusendorff and was surrendered to his numerous admirers.

Opposition may also come from the audience in the examination of the candidate. Any holder of the degree sought or any student may attack the thesis. And it is not uncommon for an opponent to appear in the audience. Last November the chief physician of a large hospital submitted what was described as "a beautiful and impressive book" dealing with the causes and the treatment of varicose veins. The clinical part of it was pronounced exceptionally good. There was a large audience present at the examination. One of the official opponents stated that the study was fully worthy of the degree but "your book," said he to the candidate, "does not give one the impression of a startling science. But you have performed a diligent and deep work, a work which we need and which had to be done."

Then there arose from the audience an opponent whose criticism was both unpleasant and arrogant. "You have made many beautiful discoveries which you do not even yourself seem to understand. Besides, you lack in your book a chapter describing the symptoms. Varicose veins are a physiological phenomenon and their problem cannot be resolved in a histological manner. This you would have understood if you had but five minutes discussed it with Professor Krogh."

There is nothing hidden or esoteric about the doctor's examination, it will be seen. It is always open to the public which has the opportunity to see the standards of scholarship exacted by the university of those who would seek the highest academic distinction available in Denmark. This practice is likely to encourage learning and respect for it. Moreover, such exercises become in themselves educational in character. The audience learns a great deal during the two or three hours' disputation over a new study even though it may be technical. Moreover, the custom is yet further proof that the Danes employ to the maximum all educational resources at their command. They pursue learning. Education seems to be the star of their life, and they are proud of their schools in which they have such sincere and unaffected confidence.

CHAPTER XIV

COMMENCEMENT EXERCISES

RECTOR Magnificus Frederik Torm, of the University, thoughtfully afforded the opportunity to attend the *Aarsfest* which is a sort of commencement occasion and benefactors' or founders' day consolidated into one grand festival. But there is really nothing very festive about the celebration. The invitation was very formal. It requested the invited guest to wear full evening dress although the exercises were to be held at two o'clock in the afternoon, in the great festival hall of the ancient institution. This room is among the first of the proud places a visitor at the university has pointed out to him, if by chance he is conducted by an alumnus who has what in America is known as chronic college spirit. A few Danes have the affliction. The room is rectangular in shape, with very high ceiling, gallery, and choir loft, and is richly possessed of mural paintings of historical and allegorical themes. On the right from the front entrance is the royal box and facing it on the other side is the rector's dais or lecture stand.

"What is the room used for?" The question was put to Dr. Vincent Naeser, a most enthusiastic alumnus of the university. He is a delightful man, one of the most distinguished Danes of the present, and he is marked by energy and keenness, a fine sense of humor, and high humanistic ideals. During a crowded morning he had moved so fast here and there that he heard from his guest the warning that in New York he would be arrested for speeding. He is altogether the most dynamic Dane yet encountered. He moved rapidly, first to his mother's old patrician residence, a palatial place, where his distinguished father had begun and Dr. Naeser and his brother now continue rather marvelous historical and archæological collections. Mrs. Andersen, the caretaker, had been there in the house just fifty-two years and she looked good for another half century Then the plant of his great paper must be inspected, *The Berlingske Tidende*, the oldest paper in Europe; and then he led the way on to the university where lunch was served. All the time Dr. Naeser talked modestly but with much spirit of his work in the interest of the International Federation of Students (an organization, by the way, which American students had not yet entered, it was pointed out) and of the International Committee of Danish Students, of which he is president, and of other influences which may in time help to bring about a warless world.

"What is the room used for?" he was asked at the festival hall. "Used. That's the right word," he replied. It is not used as much as it should be," he explained, as he talked intimately of each of the great paintings which the room contained. "Well," said he, with a twinkle and playfulness in his eyes and voice, "it is used for great university occasions, but particularly for the *Aarsfest*, which you shall attend. Over there will sit the king and over here the rector of the university. In the loft will be the students' choir, and in the galleries there will be guests and spectators. Here on the main floor and on these places around the walls will be seated the especially invited guests, the faculty of the university, and others of the intellectual and social aristocracy of the kingdom. They will all be in evening clothes, bedecked, bejewelled decorated in stars and stripes, and they will all scowl and stare at each other, as if they are bored to death, and they will yawn, and go to sleep while the rector makes a speech."

"Dr. Naeser!" exclaimed a young woman, the third member of the party, the daughter-in-law of one and the wife of another university professor, herself very highly intellectual, devoted to the noble traditions of her renowned alma mater in whose spirit and lore she is thoroughly saturated. She looked at Dr. Naeser as if he were guilty of frightful blasphemy and should be punished.

It was two weeks later that the invitation came to attend the *Aarsfest* which had been described. It did not promise to be riotous and tumultuous in festive spirit. But it should be seen. The invitation was rather disturbing in its formal demand for evening clothes. The visitor had traveled light to Denmark. A dinner jacket or tuxedo was the nearest to formal clothes that he could exhibit, unless he should rent or borrow and this would not be correct. To enter the festival hall of the great university in a rented garment? Never! It would be academic sacrilege. Besides, it seemed such a stupid demand, so altogether ridiculous. The university should change the custom, and a beginning must be made. The embarrassment was tactfully explained to the rector magnificus who urged desperate effort to acquire the proper clothes, but he was altogether reasonable about it. Would it be really dangerous not to go as commanded, the visitor asked himself. Would the consequences be serious? Would he be shot by the royal guard before daylight and without one more cup of delicious Danish coffee? "Experiment, take the risk," whispered some imp scornful of academic form. The risk was taken. The visitor went in tuxedo and neither he nor the many others in similar attire were ejected from the great festival hall.

Commencements in the United States are usually gala affairs, often quite lively, and always cheerful and hopeful in ceremony. They are times of rejoicing and of thanksgiving, students and teachers generally grateful that each are now for a season rid of the other. But it is not this way at the University of Copenhagen, where the *Aarsfest* comes right in the middle of the term's work. It is a very serious occasion. For a two hours' season of frigid formality and stifling solemnity its fellow could not possibly be found in all academic Christendom.

The guests were led to chairs carefully marked with their full names and academic or other properly certificated status, or they found their places by the aid of a diagram card which had accompanied the invitation. On the chairs were elaborate programs of the cantata which the excellently trained students' choral society later rendered with great effect,—resonant, sonorous, tuneful, as is practically all Danish music. Much of it praised the king, and he sat through it all quite calmly. The visitor wondered how it feels to have songs sung in your own praise before a discriminating though patriotic audience. He had but little basis for comparison. The nearest was to be found in American collegiate athletic events when some muttonhead tags another at third base and those in the grandstand or stadium rise with becoming adoration and to the inquiry:

"What's the matter with Jimmie?" fittingly respond: "He's all right." The students at the University of Copenhagen, however, think highly of their king if one can judge from the songs they sing about him and in his praise.

The king of Denmark is the tallest and one of the most popular of all European monarchs, and he certainly is a human person. Shortly after Parliament met in early October of last year he went over to Norway and Sweden to hunt with some other kings. Later he returned to find Denmark and Copenhagen, even the parliament house, quite as he had left them. By such an arrangement as this King Christian the Tenth not only gets some good shooting in congenial company but he escapes the necessity of having to see the newspapers which contain the speeches of the lawmakers. Moreover, it is not a breach of good manners for the king to leave town when they arrive. His political fences are kept in good repair all the time. He does not have to worry about votes, nor does he have to consider the effect of a hunting holiday on his candidacy for the United States Senate. But imagine the governor of Texas during the meeting of the legislature in her state, running off, to accept of her excellency, the governor of Wyoming, the invitation: "Come over, Ma Ferguson, and I shall put you in touch with a good dressmaker." Or, suppose the governor of South Carolina should wire during the general assembly of North Carolina to the executive of that State: "Come over, Angus: it's a long time between shots." If the Tar Heel governor should accept the invitation, the legislature would probably resent it, and he would return fully expecting to find that somebody had stolen the statehouse and had abandoned it down in Crabtree Creek. There certainly is a lot of difference to be found among rulers. Some of them take their jobs very seriously.

The king of Denmark is otherwise human. He likes his afternoon nap. If he did not take part of it in the great festival hall, right in the face of the rector's speech, and if his royal highness, Prince Knud (Canute), did not give a tender but firm princely punch in the paternal side to awaken his majesty, then the North Carolinian present needs to have his eyes examined. It did appear to him that the king went to sleep, just as a regular king should. The rector's speech may have been a trifle anesthetic, as commencement speeches so often are, and so critics should not frown too severely upon the frailty of the king.

Two handsome young university students wearing scarlet regalia ushered in the faculty, more than one hundred of the most distinguished looking professors the visitor had ever seen, more mature looking than most American college and university professors. The audience stood while the learned men took their places. Then came the king, Prince Knud, and Princes Harold and Gustav, brothers of the king, led likewise by two students also in scarlet regalia. The four young ushers then took their places in statuesque manner, two in front of the royal box and two in front of the rector's stand, and if they moved the slightest, during the fifteen minutes required for the first part of the cantata, it was not discernible to the naked eye. Four youths alive and awake were never quieter, more undisturbed or undisturbing. If American college students were all of this kind many administrative problems in higher education in that country could be solved more easily.

The retiring rector gave an address. His chair is theology and it was natural that he should choose a subject from that or some closely related field. From the few words understood and from the newspaper accounts dug out the following morning with the aid of lexicons, it was evident that the rector compared what was thought thirty or forty years ago and now in regard to certain New Testament writings. He pointed out the extreme opinions on the subject. Some people deny the historic Christ, he noted, while others take literally everything in the Bible. He gave a brief summary of certain results of scholarship which throw light on the subject, and near the conclusion used the word *udvikling* (evolution), and there was not a hiss in the hall.

The remainder of the exercises were not unlike those of American college commencements. Gold medals were presented by the rector to nine students who had during the year distinguished themselves in productive scholarship. The names of the new doctors were read, twenty-five of them, and they all stood clad in full evening clothes. The only honorary degree was conferred upon Knud Johan Victor Rasmussen, the explorer. The rector congratulated the new doctors *"i en velformet lille Tale"* (in an appropriate little speech, according to the newspapers), on their attainments, and admonished them to continue their scholarly pursuits. In the list of doctors was the name of Aage Brusendorff, whose doctor's disputation or examination the last of October had drawn such a large crowd of witnesses.

The rector then spoke appreciatively of the

retiring professors, referred to the new physiological laboratory just established, thanked the donors who were present, and spoke briefly of the increased attendance on university instruction which might call for a new institution to be set up in Jutland. This question of a new university was a very vital one in Denmark at that time. Then he spoke a few hearty words to the new rector, Dr. J. Fibiger, of the medical faculty, whom the university professors had selected to head the institution during the coming year. The installation ceremony was very simple and impressive. The retiring rector took from his own neck a gold chain bearing a medallion of Minerva and this he placed around the neck of his successor who was, by this simple act, invested with all the privileges and the high distinction of the most honorable and authoritative position in the gift of his eminent colleagues. For it is a great honor to be rector of the University of Copenhagen, or chancellor, or president, as the office is known in the United States, the more so since the selection is made by colleagues and co-workers. They seem much more competent to select a leader than are groups of ecclesiastics, politicians, or bankers, whose chief functions as educational boards of trustees should be to find funds and march in the parade at commencement. To serve as rector of the University of Copenhagen seems to be an irksome task, however, so Dr. Torm, the retiring rector, stated when he talked one afternoon earlier of university life and activities. It is not an administrative post, as in the colleges of the United States, where it often kills off many good men and furnishes havens of rest for quite as many incompetent ones. The rectorship in the University of Copenhagen is a representative position. The rector represents the university with the students, in the city, in court and diplomatic circles, and abroad if necessary, and generally he must be at home in many languages.

The exercises concluded with the chorus singing "*Vort Hjem, du danske Jord,*" (Our Home, the Danish Soil). The king shook hands with the retiring and with the new rector and then with each of the new doctors. The royal party then retired and the 446th annual commencement of the University of Copenhagen passed into history.

But what solemn history it had become! From the beginning to the end there was not the slightest applause at any statement or announcement, nor a smile, but instead the most dreadful stillness and awful solemnity marked every single moment. To a North Carolinian accustomed to prolonged applause at the mention of some theory of government, or some ideal of life, or the name of some dead politician canonized by time and forgetfulness into a statesman, it was a perfectly dreadful, torturous two hours. At any moment it would have been a relief to him to rush madly through the dead decorations up to the space between king and rector and, shedding coat, lead a vigorous yell: "One, two, one, two,—king, king, king! Copenhagen, Copenhagen, Copenhagen! Rector Torm, Rector Torm, Rector Torm! Rah, rah, rah ! ! ! " And then he would have liked to announce a baseball game between the faculty and the new doctors, Brusendorff pitching for the youngsters (though the average of the new doctors was above thirty-five years) and Jespersen, his master, on the mound for the faculty. But who would dare desecrate the great hall with words and behavior so empty and frivolous?

The Danes have been able to preserve their academic and scholarly individuality. The fact is reflected in such occasions as the *Aarsfest*. These old customs, like the ancient buildings of the university, reveal an intensity of life which both have all these years contained. The differences noted in this academic occasion, when compared with corresponding celebrations familiar to Americans, are just other differences of nations. It would be a flat world of irritating sameness if all that differentiates nations and peoples were wiped out and changed to one monotonous and drab-colored surface. It would be a dreary place if all the world were one neutral tableland without the mountains above and the valleys below. People should then become one-eyed, and miss the many-sided view which variety in forms of life and of living, and in the customs and practices and habits of peoples are likely to give. The individuality of the Danes lends charm and beauty to their culture and gives it a color of healthfulness and well-being. It is a source of their strength, a measure of their will to live, and through it they continue to contribute to the civilization of the world. This little people of the north refuse to dig their own graves by allowing their individuality to be flattened out; and in this view they fling out yet another little gleam of light to their sisters over the waters everywhere.

But it could be wished that their annual commencement exercises might have less of solemn formality,—that the Danes would smile a while.

CHAPTER XV

Respect for Learning

TO any who may have been generous and courageous enough to follow these notes to this point it must now be evident that they make no pretense at being a record of adventure or a guide to tourists. Interest has been not only in some of those things which any visitor to Denmark, under the competent guidance of a Baedeker, may see; but also in the somewhat fugitive, perhaps mystic, yet quite solid aspects of the life of this country which is one of the oldest, one of the smallest, and yet one of the most cultivated and highly developed nations of all Europe. If a little of the interior view of Danish life is properly presented through these notes American readers may find new European friends to think about and later perhaps to visit and move among if they are ever so happy in the privilege. But these notes are not for the ultra-sophisticated and sagacious readers, or the professional globe-trotters, or for any of these or others who incline to laugh at zeal about poetry and freedom and other sustained illusions of life.

What is the inner spirit of Denmark, the most subtle of the trio of Scandinavian lands? One often asks also if it is really too highly civilized. But equally as pertinent a question concerns the condition of culture among the Danes. During the brief opportunity afforded for observing them the English had appeared sanguine. But these Danes seem positively infatuated. Does one question the function and the real value of the small nations in the civilization of the world, whether they justify their independent existence, a view of the Danes interest in real education and their deep and reverent respect for scholarship and sound learning would be quite sufficient to remove any doubt whatever.

In America we have urged upon us, often with wearisome and even irritating insistence, the alleged advantages of quantity. The view is almost peculiarly American. It appears on every hand and at almost every turn. In the newspapers just now reaching Scandinavia from North Carolina appear accounts of the size of the enrollment in the various colleges, and the increase over last year, five years, ten, and fifteen years ago. It is a kind of publicity which reflects a mania for numbers and becomes for that reason a species of educational boorishness which trustees, administrators, alumni, faculty, and students take as a matter of course and seem to require as a part of the necessary propaganda in higher education. When the view is detached it all seems so artificial and unimportant. The numerical size of a student body really matters little. It is not particularly important even in athletics, for which Europe thinks so many American colleges are primarily maintained, except of course to swell the cheering and to lengthen the snake dance after the athletic games. Says one report: "Eight thousand people witnessed the University of North Carolina-Wake Forest football game," and it might have been added: "and fully half of them wished that they had not."

Apparent emphasis on education in Denmark is in somewhat striking contrast with the apparent emphasis on organized athletics in high school and college in the United States, and the notorious evils which often attend or follow. It is a difference which is forced upon the attention of an American visitor, if he is more or less familiar with educational conditions in his country and views schools in Denmark. The administrator of the University of Copenhagen, if a comparison may be permitted for the moment, can report the number of students who are enrolled there and the faculty in which each is reading. But he does not regard the information as at all important, certainly not so important as the intellectual interests of the students. These are daily demonstrated and stand altogether on their own, needing no publicity whatever. But it must not be assumed that these interests are encouraged or developed to the detriment of other worthy purposes and interests of youth. The Danish students have many other interests, but they approach their intellectual activities, which are the dominating ones, with life, and energy, and earnestness, and not languidly and with apology. It is another reflection of the universal respect for scholarship and devotion to learning which is in so much evidence in Denmark. The porter in a little hotel (this functionary corresponds to the clerk in American hotels) yesterday greatly regretted that duties at the desk kept him from going over to the University of Copenhagen at four in the afternoon to hear Professor Boas of Columbia University give his concluding lecture (in English, of course) on the languages and customs of the American Indians. And the night man in the same position was today seen busily engaged in the spacious and crowded reading room of the Royal Library. The Danes are busy readers and they have great respect for books.

The schools have given the people the habit and the desire to read. The purpose of the Danish school is to teach,—boys and girls, and men and women. Public funds in most generous amounts are provided by local and national governments to promote this purpose. "It costs a lot of money," the Danish citizen says, but he invariably adds: "but it is worth all that it costs, when one remembers what Denmark was fifty or seventy-five years ago and sees what the country is today, prosperous and educated and happy, and when one knows that it is the school and education that have worked this great change in behalf of the people."

This is a testimony that is almost a boast, if the Danes were in the least inclined to display vaingloriously or to speak with unbecoming confidence in their efforts to provide education for their children. The testimony comes not from the ministry of education in Frederiksholms Kanal in Copenhagen, or from the superintendent of schools in the *Raadhuset* in that city, or from the superintendents of schools in the provincial towns and cities. It is the universal testimony of the man in the street and in the field who is proud of his schools and the Danish system of education from top to bottom. Moreover, the rank and file of the Danish people do not look with scorn and distrust on higher education as they so often do in the United States. Education of all degrees is respected and encouraged by everybody. Even the Danish woman who advertises rooms and board proudly tells the foreign applicant that "in my country everybody can read and write, everybody," shaming him from the land of the free and the home of the brave which is not yet free enough or brave enough to bring light to thousands of illiterates. The North Carolinian recalled that in his own state there were nearly one hundred thousand white adults who could not read and write their own names, and he thought of the difficulty of having full liberty and complete equality in a community like that.

One hundred thousand illiterates, a veritable army, still in ignorance under a free and enlightened government which they would love better if it had done better by them. Shades of Horace Mann, of Henry Barnard, of Caleb Mills, of Calvin H. Wiley, of Joseph Caldwell, viewing the exigencies of politics and the energy of politicans in altering school laws and in giving them the color of pious aspiration rather than that of settled policy! How can governing authority in any American state permit to pass their lips such empty words and phrases of mockery as "liberty," "equality of opportunity," so long as such a host of their fellows sit in darkness, in servitude to ignorance, poor in civic possessions, reduced by struggles which the equity of heaven should have spared them? "We Love Our Land," sing all the Danes, and they swell with pride in their educational and cultural possessions, and boast of them as Californians boast of their climate or Carolinians of the denim mills and cotton factories. Give any American state such possessions and she too will boast and be proud of and support the cause of enlightenment. Until then, heaven's blessings attend her!

The original purpose of the school, as far back as recorded history goes, was to teach. The Danes have not diverted or deviated from it. The major duty of the Danish school still is to teach. It expends little effort in developing and exhibiting athletic teams or theatrical or musical organizations. This kind of activity the Danes do not consider education, or very educative. Danish teachers do not hesitate to ask the American visitor how children in schools in his country find time for study, when they devote so much of their time and attention to so many things of apparently quite doubtful value. "When do they study?" a teacher in an elementary school asked. The Danes view education as a business, just as they consider farming, and they give attention to it six days each week for about forty weeks each year, in all grades from the first in the folk (elementary) school on through the gymnasium, a secondary school which includes about two years of work in the average American college. This long training not only affords an excellent formal education for the people, but the high order of teaching which generally is done in the schools gives them a deep regard for learning.

But the schools do not neglect physical education or training in music. Gymnastics and music are given large places in the education of the Danes. Long training and practice are given in both subjects by teachers of recognized fitness and skill in teaching. The strong bodies of the people and the widespread interest in all things musical are adequate proof of the value and the success of this part of the Danish educational system. Denmark is a musical country; and the urban musical public, especially that of Copenhagen, is the most critical in all Europe. But even there the great kindness of the people leads them to entertain hospitably an indifferent artist who might chance to need a bit of sympathy. The numerous music stores, concerts, festivals, all attest the devotion of the Danes to this ennobling heritage now denied so many boys and girls in America which, a great artist has said, is only six years old musically.

An ordinary class in gymnastics or music at a Danish high school, especially at a teachers' college—which trains teachers for the folk schools—would compare favorably with the exhibitions of gymnastic teams or the dress performances of glee clubs in many American colleges. All the students, not a picked few, participate and become competent in these activities. It was inspiring to a North Carolinian who went to one altogether unannounced, but he was at the same time made to feel quite ashamed of the little his own state and many others in his country do to promote these valuable educational interests among the children. What bodies had these young people! And what voices! They were united—under the direction of a music master who looked the part and had been playing the part for thirty years in the same school—in moving choruses, inspiriting ballads, in Norse folk melodies, and in sonorous hymns which surely must have resembled the grandeur of the ancient Scandinavian sagas. This is a part of the training which Denmark gives to those who go out to teach little children how to take care of their bodies and how to sing. Is it any wonder that the Danes are well formed and good looking and that they love music and respect it and live in part by it?

It was at this teachers' college that the visitor

met his first real embarrassment. He had asked to see the work in music and was led to the music room where the teacher was then instructing a half hundred young men who were preparing to teach in the folk schools. Through the principal of the school, who spoke some English, the teacher said: "Perhaps our distinguished visitor would coöperate with us in showing him how my first-year class can sing. If he will go to the blackboard and write on it the music of some song which he knows but which my class does not know, I shall show him how readily and easily the class can sing it, and how well." The visitor explained that this he could not do. "Perhaps, then, our distinguished visitor will select from this book of English songs a song which the class does not know." He selected "My Old Kentucky Home." A student went to the blackboard and wrote the music; and in ten minutes the class, which had never seen or heard it before, was singing it quite as well as it could be sung by a group of American college students who knew it well.

And the Danish teachers teach. As noted elsewhere they are all well trained for their work. The average high school teachers, whose training is quite equal to and whose skill in the art exceeds that of most American college professors, teach from twenty-four to twenty-seven class periods a week, usually about forty-five minutes in length. The teachers in the university and in the teachers' colleges and other higher institutions which abound in Denmark regard teaching as their first great care. They do not spend their time mewed up in committee rooms evolving rules and regulations, soon to be repealed for others, to enable some indifferent student who does not know why he is there to substitute a few points in French for a few in German, neither of which he learns to speak—because for some unaccountable reason the American schools and colleges generally do not teach their students to speak foreign languages and seldom to read them very well—or to excuse such an indifferent student from this or that under this or that condition. Danish teachers do not waste precious time in formulating rules in committee or in faculty meetings, butting prepositions and commas out of such rules in order to afford emergency protection to some cake eater who thinks he can play football or sing bass or play end man in a minstrel show. And yet in America this is important. For with no cake eaters or minstrels, American colleges would have to adjourn many of their alumni meetings and most of their so-called college spirit.

It would be difficult to imagine the lively, energetic, vigorous-minded university and college students in Denmark "splitting Copenhagen" for some athletic team from Lund or Stockholm, even though they are the most courteous students you will find anywhere. Nor could they sing "Hark, the Sound of Viking Voices," or "Fair Copenhagen" and then go to their rooms and write home about it. This is nothing to write home about, the chapel talks of college deans and presidents to the contrary notwithstanding. These college officials are in reality under no illusion about these and certain other conditions which so often surround American education, but what can they do about it? The handbook of the University of Copenhagen says nothing about a yell, because the students have all passed the yelling period. Danish students do not even select rhythmic mottoes or class flowers. They go about their school and college work, just as their elders go about their divorces, seriously, with a strange admixture of energy and stolid acquiescence, but they, like their elders, display an admirably balanced averageness about it all and seldom, in this or other activities, do they rise to great heights or sink to great depths.

There are many other evidences of the Danish respect for schools and learning. They constantly appear: because it requires no profusion of good luck for a visitor to get right inside the life of these people, in city and country, into the homes of many of them. They lay themselves out with zeal to serve him through most delicate invitations to this and to that. And the view that the visitor gets from these intimate contacts leads always to the reflection that a school, or a college or a university, just like a nation, must concentrate all its energies on quality if it is to become and remain dignified, estimable, and effective in the civilization which it is set up to minister to and to serve. In this is to be found one of Denmark's distinctions, if it may now be pointed out again. There is a peculiar mode of thought here, an extraordinary mental activity, a quite distinguished personal outlook on life, produced largely by the kind of education which the people believe in whole-heartedly and support freely and in such great abundance. It is real education the Danes have. They are infatuated with confidence in and respect for it, an attitude that is as admirable as it is impressive to a visitor from a community where learning and education might well be held in greater esteem.

But for a North Carolinian of Scotch and a strain of Quaker ancestry to commend fully all the Danish views and ways of life would be to mistrust slightly the evidence of his own experience and training, or to deny the validity of certain institutions which are stronger in sanction and respect where rationalism is less rampant than here or where it assumes less grotesque forms. There are apparent weaknesses in Danish life, to be indicated later, but it is doubtful if they can be properly charged to the school system. There are points in this which might be strengthened perhaps without doing violence to its essential structure. But more of this later. Meantime, he does commend to his fellows in the United States the Danish respect and reverence for and confidence in the power of real education.

CHAPTER XVI

EDUCATION AND AGRICULTURE

THE Athenians must have been bored by hearing so much about the virtues of Aristides the Just, quite as less advanced farming sections tire at hearing the praises of Denmark, if they by any chance tune in when such songs are sung. For the Danish system of agriculture has been viewed, studied, written and spoken about very favorably, often even glorified, by individuals, commissions, and delegations from far and near, who have made the little country appear almost a rural Utopia. And people continue to come in great numbers, but the Danes smile at the brevity of some of the visits and the length of some of the reports which follow those who seem feverishly to seek the secret by which the country has been converted from a poor into a prosperous place as if by magic.

To one who lays no claim to expertness in agricultural economics the magic seems to have been education, in the broad as well as the technical sense, much and many kinds of education, and available in abundance for the many needs of rural life. For Denmark is rural. Eighty per cent of the country is under profitable agriculture, and altogether Denmark is only one-third the size of North Carolina or of New York, twice the size of Massachusetts, one-fourth the size of Iowa, and about one-twentieth the size of Texas. But she supports a population of about three and a half million and sells millions in produce to help feed others, especially her English cousins across the North Sea. This rural prosperity education has helped to make,— seems indeed in large part to have made. The various land laws have had marked influence of course, especially since 1899, by helping to make of Denmark a commonwealth of small and medium-sized agricultural properties. But this legislation, simple in its arrangements and seemingly quite equitable in the main, is also a product of education.

Education seems to be the mainspring of Denmark's progress in almost all directions. Education has taught the Danes to know and to recognize the need of a method that is standardized to suit each problem in farming. Men are trained to be farmers. In the numerous agricultural colleges—the latest report of the ministry of education shows twenty-one such schools—the students are selected for their experience in agriculture, and in winter courses they learn the theory underlying the practice of their occupation. By education and training they become equipped not only with manual dexterity but with a social sympathy that fits them to coöperate with their fellows. The teachers in these schools have had fuller courses in the theory and practice of farming and the whole system works in with and not apart from agriculture. With their minds enriched the students return to the land instead of being divorced from it. Life on the farm is made attractive, and agriculture is viewed as a progressive science. Their high standard of technical education is but a corollary to their desire for such education, to be gained, however, not to enable them to leave the land but to live better on it. They avail themselves of expert and technical advice and then they apply it to the improvement of their business: to the development, the feeding, and the housing of domestic animals, to the improvement of varieties of cultivated plants, and to profitable ways of production and distribution. The organization of all this work is initiated and built up by the people themselves: the collective purchasing of raw materials, the manufacturing and marketing of their products, and even the press service which broadcasts home and foreign technical and trade information from one end of the active country to the other. The Danes go about farming as a big business. Self-help in its highest sense is assuredly the principle which has enabled the Danish farmers to attain their remarkable success. The schools have so taught them.

This chapter deals with a kind of education in Denmark that is badly needed and very scarce in most of the American states. It concerns the subject of agricultural education, which falls quite within the interest of the visitor who may perhaps be permitted a word about it here. The twenty-one agricultural colleges in Denmark have so much to do with farming that agriculturalists in the United States should know about them. It may amaze them, however, to learn that these twenty-one institutions for farmers and their sons and daughters, in a territory one-third the size of North Carolina or one-fourth the size of Iowa, have not a single football team, military band, or class yell. American agriculturalists may have learned something when they learn this fact. But those who may chance to read this are under no obligation to read further in this note, because the visitor's introduction to Danish agricultural education and his acquaintance with the ways of life among some Danish agriculturalists may be so intimate and personal as to seem inappropriate in a public report.

At a pleasant party in a charming home in Copenhagen last December a North Carolinian was included among the guests whose manners impressed him as remarkably urbane and townish, with nothing of the rural or rustic about them. Toward the end of the evening a somewhat stiff and young Danish officer, who looked as if he had been poured in a molten state into his brilliant uniform, approached with his sister, clicked his heels together and politely inquired if the visitor from North Carolina was interested in agriculture. Interest in agriculture was promptly admitted. A civilian should never argue with a soldier. "Then we should be so happy," said the young soldier, "to have you spend some days with us on our little farm. We bring the invitation to you from our father and mother. I regret that my duty in the guard shall keep me here in the city while you visit my family in the country."

The young officer's manner was so mild and there was such an absence of that indescribable hauteur which one generally associates with military officers of all kinds, conditions, and ranks, and his sister was so delightful, that they put at instant ease the timid foreigner across whose lips not a Danish sentence had been able to stagger during the entire evening. But he was a trifle hesitating because it was not then clear just how decided educational advantages could be gained by a visit to a small Danish farm. The impulse was to go, however, and so the invitation was very courteously if somewhat tentatively accepted for Saturday of the next week, the foreigner resolving upon an investigation meantime complete and thorough enough to establish the size and importance of the farmer and his farm.

The investigation was not to prolong itself. The following day the consul general of the United States discharged his duty to the government which had sent him to Denmark and had the North Carolinian at his club for lunch. The invitation to the farm was noted and the name of the family was mentioned. "It's one of the noblest names in Denmark," the polite general assured his guest, who interpreted that to mean merely that no member had been convicted of breaking a bank, of defaulting as treasurer of the state or of a Sunday school, or was under a cloud of suspicion of political party disloyalty. The consul general of the United States comes from the solid South where a gentleman is always expected to be the kind of gentleman he is always expected to be.

On Friday came a telephone message that the farmer and his wife had been called to Copenhagen; he, it was later learned, to attend a called meeting of a bank's directors and she to be present at the birthday celebration of some relative. Birthdays are important events in Denmark and are generally very carefully observed by all classes. Over the telephone it was intimated that inasmuch as the daughter and her week-end guest, an attractive young woman from Copenhagen, would be alone on the farm, it might be more conventional for the gentleman from North Carolina to come down the following week when the parents should have returned. They should regret not to see him. The idea seemed reasonable and altogether safe and chaste enough. Other plans must be made for the days intervening before the journey to the farm should begin. But early Saturday morning came another telephone message that after a family conference the farmer and his wife saw no reason why "you should not journey here tomorrow and remain until my parents return Tuesday." And this idea seemed even more sensible than the other. Why should banks and birthday parties restrict a gentleman's opportunity to study Danish agriculture? Wouldn't that be ridiculous? Viewed in retrospect it would have been very unfortunate also.

The journey was five hours from Copenhagen to the south. The visitor was to leave the train at a little railway station on a line which branches off from the principal artery of traffic between Scandinavia and continental Europe. A surprise awaited him. It was no farm hand in overalls and rickety Ford that met his gaze at the station on that crisp December day, but two charming women, young enough to teach in a rural school anywhere in the United States. They were seated in a high-powered American-built limousine, and attended by a chauffeur in livery. The front doors of the motor car and the cap of the driver bore a curious label which the visitor naturally fancied was the mark of the coöperative agricultural society of the farmer. The ten minutes' drive through an enchanting, prosperous looking rural community to the farm house, and a cup of tea and some Danish cakes immediately after arrival, served somewhat to restore the amazed visitor, who was quite unprepared for the shock of such a reception. Who were these people anyway?

The farmhouse had been the ancestral home of the family for many generations. The farmer and his father's father and grandfather had all farmed successfully and lived happily there. Though of ancient origin, the house was as modern in all of its appointments as a New York apartment, and presented a most attractive exterior and an interior filled with books and magazines, pictures and paintings, and other suggestions of leisure and culture. It would be wearisome to describe the numerous rooms.

There was an irritating number of servants. They were not the abject and servile kind but more or less professional workers whose service was viewed by them and their employers as apprentice preparation for the management of their own homes and farms later. They were paid and treated well by their employers and fully protected in their rights by advanced social legislation. But they were harassing in numbers. There was one for every need. They shined your shoes, and pressed and looked after your clothes, and tidied up your room many times a day, and thoughtfully turned down your bed in early evening, and tenderly laid your pajamas on the pillow. They performed many other intimate services such as drawing your bath, and now and then one showed some disposition to preside at it after the manner of the Swedes. But this seemed to be carrying service too far, even beyond the ideals of Rotary.

The visitor believed that the bath is a rite which, except for children and invalids, should be celebrated without supervision or inspection. But a foreigner in Scandinavia must sooner or later learn when to dismiss the servant. They are not so persistent in Denmark, however, as they are in Sweden where the bathing facilities in hotels and other public places are in the hands of quite ceremonious attendants who are jealous of their prerogatives and part unwillingly with the least punctilio in their practices. Unless the foreigner is unable to take a bath unassisted he must learn to submit to the Swedish custom or violate it by shooing out the servants.

Those who are ever fortunate enough to visit Denmark should know also about a Danish breakfast in bed. If they have never had breakfast in bed except when they were ill, or did not want to go to work, or meet the banker who nursed their overdraft or overdue note, or to church or a college faculty meeting; if they have never had breakfast in bed in an up-to-the-last-minute farmhouse when they were perfectly free from such irritations as these, they have been deprived of a joy and a comfort that surely must have been designed away back yonder when the world and man were young.

Nothing could be more luxurious and yet so delicate and modest and unexposed to coarseness and excessive pride as breakfast in bed in a Danish farmhouse. Nothing in all the numerous attentions seemed so thoughtful and hospitable as the interest of the young Danish hostess in seeing that her guest at the farm should every morning have his breakfast in bed. The Danes may have borrowed the custom from their English cousins, among whom it seems so natural, or the English may have acquired it from the Danes when the latter bossed the British Isles. Farm life and breakfast in bed had at first seemed awkward to the visitor and quite at odds with one another, but after the first morning the luxury became for him a downright necessity.

He lived from one morning to the next in the keenest anticipation of breakfast in bed. It was so cosy and consoling. He did not have then nor does he now have any interest whatever in a premature examination of a halo and a harp and honey on a heavenly cloud, as enticing as they may seem, because he does not know how satisfactory they would be. But he does know that in removing weariness and despondency and loneliness from a spirit sore fretted with dull neutralities or tired to sickness of the janglings and nonsense noises of the wicked world about, there is probably nothing so effective, no balm so benign and healing, no solace so pleasing and diverting, no comfort whose ministration is so refreshing, no appurtenance or condition of domestic life that brings such physical and mental ease and quietude, —there is nothing in this world at least that can excel a Danish breakfast in bed.

The history of breakfast in bed cannot be gone into here, but it must date from the garden described in that guide book which was adopted by the Baptists at their convention in Texas last spring. Whatever its origin, the arrangement is certainly very satisfying and it seems orthodox enough for anybody. Think of the comforts it could be made to bring to tired college presidents and professors, their athletic teams and coaches, to school teachers and preachers, to plumbers and bankers, to doctors and lawyers, to weary farm women, to newspaper editors, to politicians and prowlers of other kinds, to the homeless multitude, and to the tenants and farmers whose working hours are now and then all too long but whose working days could well be lengthened.

Breakfast in bed is a valuable institution, with a place in human economy as important as party platforms, national flags and national anthems, commencement speeches, and Kiwanis. "God Save the King" and breakfast in bed have made England the great nation she is, quiet, dignified, deliberate. Nothing but breakfast in bed could have settled the general English strike last May. If England should extend the custom and permit it in Ireland the problems of home rule would be simple, and all the bloody struggles could be settled in a fortnight. Nothing yet tried could so promptly humanize, modernize, charm and sooth the disaffected in society and put them at peace with the world in which they live and are allowed a living—as breakfast in bed.

The first morning, after breakfast in bed, the farm was inspected and afterwards two small but excellent rural schools, a near-by rural church and library were visited. The young hostess led the way first to the barn and stables where the blooded cattle and stock were cared for by men who were trained in agricultural colleges for the purpose. The hundred or more beautiful cows in stalls spotlessly clean and comfortable made a picture such as the visitor had never yet seen. The inspection tour then led through many parts of the farm. All the time the hostess talked interestingly of farming in all its aspects, of chemistry, and botany, and zoölogy, the care, selection and cultivation of plants with regard to their economic value, of coöperative buying and selling of farm products, and of the work of Denmark's agricultural colleges.

In her mind agriculture and home-making were the worthiest callings of man, and in the mind of her guest she raised agriculture to as dignified a position as medicine, law, the ministry, engineering, or teaching. "Our agricultural schools became effective," she noted, "when the basic arts upon which the future welfare of Danish life depends were given their proper place side by side with the so-called traditional subjects. They have helped to raise the condition of the farmers and of farming in the minds of the people, have made farming as great an avenue to distinction as politics and," with emphasis in her voice, "these schools have led public opinion in Denmark to give as much consideration to the man who does things as was formerly too often given to the man who only talked about doing them." She showed familiarity with farming in England, France, and Germany, knew something of farming in the United States, and was almost as much at home in the languages of these countries as she was in her own or the language of modern agriculture.

One of these colleges must be visited, and the opportunity came the following day. It was one of the oldest of the score or more such institutions in Denmark and there a North Carolinian saw what agricultural education of the right kind can do for a people. The buildings and grounds were of the most attractive kind and the lecture rooms and laboratories and library were filled with the best teachers, research directors, and materials. The school was set in the midst of a large farm which was actually used for laboratory and experimental purposes by the carefully picked students under most expert direction. The students had finished the elementary school, had had two or three years' experience in practical agriculture, had probably attended a folk high school, and some of them had had training at the gymnasium schools and perhaps at the University as well.

Then they were ready for their systematic and theoretic and further practical study of chemistry, organic and inorganic, fertilizers, physics, the treatment of soils, the rotation of crops, plant and seed culture, plant diseases, breeding and care of domestic animals, horseshoeing and smithing, dairying, farm accounting, farm machinery, surveying and leveling, arithmetic, history of agriculture, Danish language and composition. Courses in sociology and economics were also found. And there were many practical exercises required of the students whose activities seemed very business-like and somewhat exacting.

Last year there were about 1800 young men in the Danish agricultural colleges and about 500 young women in schools of domestic science and household economics, where hygiene and sanitation, gymnastics, accounting, history, music and song, physics and chemistry, housekeeping and house management, hand work, sick and child nursing, practical household accounting, plant culture, domestic animals, and similar subjects were studied. In addition to these schools the Danes have also provided numerous short courses for farmers and farm workers of all kinds.

At the head of all these institutions established to give agricultural instruction and training stands the Royal Veterinary and Agricultural College in the heart of Copenhagen, with a faculty of nearly a half hundred professors and instructors and 500 students. This may be called the mother school of Danish agricultural education. It began its work about the time the thirteen American Colonies were gaining their independence from England. From quite simple beginnings it has from time to time expanded until today it is one of the important agricultural research institutes in the world. Experimentation, research, and instruction are promoted in agriculture, horticulture, dairying, forestry, surveying, and veterinary science. Admission, which is not limited to Danes, is open to all who have had a certain practical training acquired outside the institution and who have the necessary educational preparation such as the student's or other examinations show. The courses range in length from nearly three to more than five years. Forestry, a very important subject to the Danes, includes two years of practical forest service and the work in surveying requires one year of practice.

This school, which the Danes always desire foreigners to visit, is the center and source of Denmark's agricultural activities and studies. It is highly scientific in nature and function. Here the teachers in the twenty-one local agricultural colleges in the rural communities have had their training. Numerous research laboratories liberally subsidized by public funds are essential parts of the equipment where many agricultural and economic experiments,—chemical, bacteriological, physiological,—in dairying, feeding, and breeding of cattle, swine, and poultry are conducted at selected farms here and there throughout the country. Continuous tests of butter and other dairy products intended for export are here directed; and various kinds of serum, vaccines, and other preventives of diseases among domestic animals are prepared, manufactured, and dis-

ANOTHER VIEW OF ASKOV FOLK HIGH SCHOOL

tributed. Numerous experts in agricultural economics are connected with the college whose work is closely related to that of the ministry of agriculture, the ministry of justice, and the experiment farms which dot the Danish Kingdom. These experts also assist the local agricultural colleges, give advice through them to farmers, and in many other ways stimulate interest in agricultural improvement.

The State College of Engineering which dates from 1829 also occupies an important place in the Danish agricultural and educational system. Here chemical motive power, civil and electrical engineering and their many different branches and specialties are pursued by more than twelve hundred students under more than a half hundred expert teachers and research directors. Preparation is required in the mathematical-scientific line of the gymnasium, as shown by passing the rigid students' examination. The entering students in this school, therefore, have had about the equivalent of two years of American college work. The courses which they pursue range in length from nearly five to six and often seven years before the diploma (candidate in polytechnics) is gained. The graduates of this institution are excellently trained and many of them follow their professions successfully at home and abroad. The traditions from the time of Oersted, the famous discoverer of electro-magnetism, are still held in great honor and reverence and the standard of teaching appears to be very high. The school is equipped with many excellent research laboratories.

In addition to the college of engineering there is also the Technological Institute in Copenhagen, founded in 1908 for the purpose of promoting technical skill among artisans and small manufacturers. There is a division for each trade. There were enrolled here last year 3500 students. Other technical schools numbering 257 are found in the Danish towns and rural districts with 25,000 students, a fact which is likely to amaze any visitor from any American state.

The thoroughness and the excellence of the system of agricultural and industrial training in Denmark are unsurpassed by the many larger industrial countries. This fact is the explanation of the high and wide recognition which the superior quality of farming in Denmark has attained. The factors which account for the high level of excellence in the economic life of that country, which is so largely rural, are the excellent system of popular education, which has done so much to raise the level of intelligence and culture among the rural people, and the special agricultural and technical schools, which are designed especially to meet the needs of workers in these fields of activity. Any man or woman of average ability finds it easy in Denmark to get whatever theoretic and practical technical training he or she may desire, even to the highest degree obtainable. In this excellent educational provision by the Danish government for the Danish people are lessons for every American state. Adequate agricultural and technical education would make not only for economic stability but also for a more satisfying civilization among the agricultural and industrial workers of the United States as these achievements have been made among the Danes.

The Danes, like most Europeans, however, still have some inadequate notions of the United States. To many of them it is in large part undeveloped and primitive. One evening after supper the conversation had turned on the United States. The young women had asked many questions about the great distances, the sizes of states and cities, and the like. A large atlas was found and the North Carolina school teacher taught his fair disciples some elementary geography of his own country. "Where do the Indians live?" one of them asked. It was explained that they had rapidly disappeared, but that most of those remaining had become civilized enough to play football and to sell real estate and fire insurance.

"How did you rest last night?" the hostess asked the young woman from Copenhagen. It was after breakfast in bed the following morning and the three had assembled in the library to read the papers and make plans for the day. "Not very well," she replied. "I was disturbed by a dream. I dreamed that I married an American and we went to live in the plains of the United States. The Indians attacked, massacred us, and burned our humble hut."

It began to look as if the time for the guest to depart from the farm was rapidly approaching. Already the suspicion, which was aroused upon his arrival,-that this was a noble farmer had been confirmed. Those queer looking labels on the car door and on the cap of the chauffeur were not the crest of a coöperative agricultural society at all but the coat-of-arms of an ancient family of the Danish nobility. Their lineage had been detailed in several pages in the *Adels Aarbog* (Danish book of nobility) examined in the library one evening before supper. The visitor had been entertained for a week on the farm of a certificated count, and a pedigreed countess had taught him agriculture in return for lessons in geography and every morning had ordered his breakfast in bed. This discovery is not reported boastfully but as evidence that at least a part of his time in Denmark was spent in proper company.

Neither this discovery nor the lady's dream of the Indian massacre hastened him away. The real reason for leaving was a fear more rational than that inspired by dreams and the Danish nobility. It was the fear of servants. He had traveled light to Denmark and lighter to the farm. In leaving Copenhagen he had been careful enough to throw into his bags a dinner jacket and its accessories which proved to be useful in the quiet evenings on the farm. But less care was observed in packing more intimate garments. One suit of pajamas was quite creditable, but the other, it was discovered when need for it arose, turned out to be the trousers of a tan colored suit and the coat of a light blue one. They clashed violently and ignobly. If the garments were locked every morning in the bag, the discerning maid would conclude that her house was entertaining a guest who had no change. If the clashing pieces were left in bed for her attention, her æsthetic nature would be outraged, and he would be an object for the hand of scorn to point her slow, unmoving finger at, as a guest in need of a change. It was this need which drove him reluctantly from this noble farm and breakfast in bed, but he left with high regard for the Danish system of agricultural education and great admiration for the esteem in which the Danes hold life on the farm.

CHAPTER XVII

Taxes

BENJAMIN FRANKLIN, shortly after the adoption of the Constitution of the United States, wrote that everything appeared to promise that it would last. But he promptly added: "But in this world nothing is certain but death and taxes." Thirty years later Sydney Smith, the English essayist and wit, wrote about the beardless youth managing his taxed horse which wore a taxed bridle on a taxed road, and the dying man pouring out his medicine, on which he had paid a tax of seven per cent, into a spoon, taxed fifteen per cent, and, flinging himself back upon his chintz bed on which he had paid a tax of twenty-two per cent, expiring in the arms of the doctor who had paid a license tax of a hundred pounds for the privilege of putting him to death.

Both Franklin and Smith reflected the ancient view that taxation is evil, as calamitous as death, to be evaded and avoided, if possible. Charles D. McIver, a North Carolina educational reformer, expressed another view, that taxation justly levied and properly applied is a mark of civilization. He noted that the savage pays no tax. If McIver was right the Danes are among the most highly civilized people on earth because they are heavily taxed and apply taxation as investments in common prosperity. The Danish view is preference for the pressure of taxation, however heavy, to any load of ignorance and the dangers which walk in its steps, however light. There are taxes in Denmark which many of the American states do not know.

Viewing the large number of social tasks which Denmark is occupying herself with, a visitor from a state nearly three times as large, with nearly the same number of people, and potentially of greater economic power, naturally wondered how that little northern country pays for all that she is doing for her people and for all that she does to enable them to do for themselves. Last year, according to published official statements, public expenditure in Denmark, state and local, amounted to nearly 750 million kroner, a sum equal to about 187 million dollars. The central government expended nearly one hundred million of this sum, which represented a three-fold increase since 1914. The revenue to meet this larger expenditure was secured by an increased income from the rise in the level of prices, by increased tax rates and by opening up new sources of taxation. But most of this public outlay the Danes regard as the sensible investments that they in reality are.

The business of government in Denmark has timely lessons for any American communities whose taxation problems are perplexing because of outworn practices or political prejudice. The Danes with marked success operate their commonwealth upon common sense principles and in the interest of all. Schools are among their first great concerns. For liberal support of education in all forms and of other welfare agencies Denmark is perhaps unsurpassed in all Europe and probably cannot be matched by any American state or smaller administrative unit. Protection of workers, restriction upon the labor of children and women, the requirement of safe hygienic and sanitary conditions of work, regulation of working hours, care of widows and orphans, care of the aged and sick, unemployment, accident, and invalidity insurance, and stringent regulation of places which trade in alcoholic beverages are subjects to which the Danes attend. For practicability and broad humanity the Danish code of social legislation is unexcelled. Between this and the general economic and educational development and wholesomeness of the country there is a very close connection. And yet the Danish government is not conducted as a charity organization.

It is not extravagant to claim that in Denmark a new political idea appears in the attempt to eliminate prejudice in politics and to conduct government by scientific methods. There one finds respect for political scientists outside their university class rooms. The Dane defers to the specialist in the management of the state as in agriculture. He has great admiration for our highly successful industrial civilization where the individual as executive is so skillful and resourceful but he is puzzled at the low estate of our politics. In general he believes, from what he reads and hears, that many of the modern American states are inefficiently and badly governed largely because the people themselves are indifferent or are influenced by their prejudices and not by common sense or intelligence in choosing their lawmakers and executives.

In Denmark a much larger percentage of the voters actually cast ballots than in most of the American states. Moreover, the people, who are generally very well educated, as a rule go to the polls with impersonal and unprejudiced views of the issues. They are not moved so much by opinions inherited from the past or accepted from the speeches or other public statements of partisan politicans or editors of party newspapers. The Danes do not regard politics as a form of warfare to be waged between or among political groups nor their parties as sacred centers of omnipotence or omniscience, as is so often the case in the United States. They consider politics rather a means of extending prosperity and well-being to all the people, through protection of the weak and the ill-favored against the strong and the well-favored, through guarding all against injustice. The Dane is more likely to inquire of an issue: "Is this good for the state, for the Danish people?" Rarely does he give first place in his thought to the effect of the issue upon the fortunes of his party. The good of Denmark comes foremost with the Danes when they go to vote. This practice has greatly stimulated and refreshed government among the Danes; and it also refutes the argument so often heard that democracy is less efficient than autocracy and dictatorship with its cruelties and hardships.

If North Carolina and other states could gain the Danish attitude on government and taxation there would be less injustice among the people. Millions of their children would not be cheated by short term schools and deadening teachers in rural communities. Reform would promptly come in taxation which in many of the states is about as vicious as it could possibly be. It now reflects an attitude which is inherited from the days when autocracy ruled and it was a life-and-death struggle for the people to gain their rights from those in control. And politicians and demagogues today, often for their own advancement, help to perpetuate the struggle. They continue to stimulate the conception that politics and government are not the means of making a better state but of keeping up partisan rivalries and warfare.

Consider, moreover, the prevalent view in some American communities that it is traitorous for people to change their party, or the practice among most of them of waiting for the announcement of party platforms before they declare their own beliefs on any issue. This is a condition which makes the political mind stagnant, lacking in imagination, loath to admit responsibility for the practical human needs of the State, indifferent to proposed reforms until they threaten to molest the party in power. Then the political mind too often becomes hostile. A fresh war ensues. It is a condition also which makes much of our government a political monasticism, and political monastics of those in authority, provincials in the geography of contemporary needs. Their vows to party negate or deny the real needs of their time as the vows of the mediaeval monk negated the needs of his. It is one of the conditions which prevent rural communities from having better schools.

Denmark is heavily but quite uncomplainingly taxed. The Danes believe in taxation as a civilizing and productive measure if properly levied and applied. They have many kinds of taxes. There is a tax on real estate which yields about two and three-quarter million dollars, a tax on personal income and on the profits of companies which brings in more than twenty million, a property tax which yields nearly eleven million, a legacy tax which yields about two million, a stamp tax which brings more than six million, and customs duties which produce more than twenty-five million. The tax on

spirits amounts to some nine million dollars and
the beer tax yields more than six million annually.
The entertainment tax, which grades from ten
per cent to forty per cent on tickets to concerts,
theatres, moving pictures, and the like, brings
about two million dollars a year. The restaurant
tax yields nearly five million dollars.

Other sources of state revenue amount to nearly
seven million and include fees and perquisites,
state properties, post office and telegraphs, national
bank, lotteries, fines and penalties. But the
government gathers only a quarter million dollars
a year from all fines and penalties. Compare the
item with that in North Carolina. All told the
revenue of the central Danish government last
year was close to ninety-seven million dollars.
Local government revenue was derived from
municipal property and public undertakings, private
property, income, and the like, and amounted
to nearly ninety-nine million dollars. Local government
expenditures were about eighty-seven
million. Expenditures of the central government
amounted to slightly above one hundred
million.

Some revenue is now received from the railway,
telegraph, telephone, and postal services, though
during and immediately following the great war
these properties showed large deficits. But in the
fiscal year 1923–1924 they showed a surplus of
nearly two million dollars. Practically half of
the railways, including all the trunk lines, are
state owned. Altogether there are some sixty
railway companies in Denmark, however, and
since 1916 there has been a growth in private
railway mileage. But the word private is not an
altogether apt description of such lines. Nominal-

ly they are operated by private companies, but nearly all the shares are owned by the State and the towns and cities. Little private capital is invested in them. A somewhat small source of revenue is the National Bank (*Nationalbanken i Copenhagen*) which has the sole right to issue notes in Denmark. Of its annual profits the government has a priority claim on 750,000 kroner, nearly $200,000. The remainder is divided in accordance with fixed rules among the government, the reserve fund, and the shareholders.

A somewhat unusual source of public revenue in Denmark is the State lottery (*klasselotteriet*) and the stamp duty on lottery tickets which yield something above a half million dollars annually. The lottery has existed among the Danes quite above a century and a half. The question of abolishing it has often been discussed but it is yet retained and defended by the government. The general view of its defenders is that if there were no genuine and well regulated lottery those people who naturally like devices of chance and will gamble might and probably would squander money in fraudulent schemes of similar kind in other European countries. Profits, if any, from such habits of the people should go to the government, says Denmark, rather than to private and often irresponsible promoters.

The national debt of Denmark amounts to 1217 million kroner, a bit more than 300 million dollars, or a per capita debt of above ninety dollars. This consists of an internal debt of 672 million kroner and a foreign debt of 545 million kroner. Since 1914 the Danish national debt has increased more than three-fold. Local government (towns and counties) have a total indebtedness of about 1000 million kroner, or 250 million dollars. Much of this total indebtedness represents capital investments in state undertakings and the acquisition of other properties. The net assets of the Danish government, including securities, cash, profit-yielding property and the like greatly exceed its liabilities. The balance sheet of local government also shows large net assets. Most municipalities have in recent years invested in and acquired ownership of many public utilities, gas, water, electricity, street railways, and the like, which in England and the United States are so often left to private initiative and control. The Danes view their government as business but much more than the business of bookkeeping.

The expenditures were made for many purposes. Of the cost of the central government less than three per cent was for the civil list (royal family), parliament, the foreign office, and legations and consulates abroad. Twelve per cent went for national defence (army and navy), about seven per cent was used to promote trade and industry, agriculture and forestry, fisheries and commerce. Fifteen per cent was applied to the national debt, and about ten per cent to interior administration, justice, prisons, etc. Practically all the other expenditures were for purposes of social betterment, schools, public health, old age pensions, unemployment, sick benefits, hospitals, science, art, and the like. The expenditures of local government (municipalities and counties) showed equally as large a part for these purposes of social welfare. The largest item was for schools.

The assessment of taxes upon the real or capital value of property, both buildings and lands, and the elimination of disproportionate and unjust burdens on the land, form one guiding principle of public finance in Denmark. Another impressive principle at work there is that of expending the greater part of the public revenue upon social and productive purposes, such as schools, health, protection of workmen, protection of persons disabled through no fault of their own, pensions, and the like, rather than upon military and unproductive purposes. The result has been the development of excellent education agencies, the rather marvelous increase in economic wealth and the enlargement and intensity of both private and public willingness to use such wealth for the common good.

An interesting source of revenue of the Danish state is the commercial traveller's license which causes, however, much trouble and inconvenience. The cost of this license, which is now the equivalent of $100, and the increased stringency with which the requirements are enforced cause numerous complaints. The government considers it a protective measure and it has the sanction of all political parties in Denmark. The Danish industrial interests and all others who hold to a strictly protective policy keenly oppose any concessions. This kind of license is very old; the Danish enactment dates from 1839. It applies to all persons travelling in Denmark to do business on behalf of a foreign firm. The main criterion in judging to whom the tax shall apply seems to be the seeking and taking of orders. As the foreign visitor naturally talks business with the Danish business men he meets it would seem natural that he would be liable for the license. But as a rule if the visitor does not book an order or permit the Danish representative to do so in the visitor's presence, he is considered free from taking out a license.

This is one way the law is evaded. With the high barriers set up by the fee exacted for the license, "smuggling" becomes quite worth while. An American representing a large automobile concern in the United States exhibited a card which described the bearer as a "research engineer" who registered as such at the hotels. An Englishman representing a mammoth jute trade registered as a "clerk." Both men were in Denmark to promote the sales of their firms but each was ingenious and ready-witted enough to enter a false description of his real identity for the scrutiny of the police. The report is that this kind of cunning goes on constantly in an effort to defeat this protection of Danish business.

Perhaps a word may be said here about the unpopular and often even obnoxious Danish restaurant tax. It is now only four or five years old but it is strong enough to bring to the government a large sum each year. Last year it was about five million dollars. It is a state tax (*statskat*) of ten per cent on all sales in all restaurants, cafes, public dining-rooms, and other eating and drinking places, but not on the letting of rooms. To the restaurant or cafe check or bill the Danish waiter calculates and adds the ten per cent. To this total sum the guest is expected to add not less than ten per cent as *drikkepenge*, the gratuity or tip for the waiter. In practice this is as obligatory as the restaurant tax. The waiter expects it and needs it, for the hotels pay him nothing. He must live entirely on his tips. He may even pay the hotels for the privilege of serving in them, though the suspicion could not be confirmed. Practically all hotel employees, the clerks, elevator operators, porters, boots, waiters, and maids depend upon tips for their visible means of support. This appeared to be one of the most degrading practices in all Scandinavia. It is found in other European countries as well. The cooks and housekeepers are paid by the hotels and the scrub-women by the floor maids.

So under the by-laws of the order of ancient, fearless, and accepting waiters the Danish members receive at least ten per cent on the bill plus the state tax, or fifteen per cent, or more, depending upon the degree of sobriety prevailing in the guest at the moment the bill is presented. In Norway the waiter adds the ten per cent tip to the bill, right in the face of the guest, as the service charge. The matter may end here unless the guest is very generous. There appeared no state tax on restaurant bills in Norway; but the Swedes employ the same method of robbery as is used in Denmark and collect the state tax on the spot.

Managing editors of the papers publishing this article should allow these statements to stand, if they are Rotarians, as warning to fellow members who may visit Scandinavia. Copenhagen has been making eyes at Rotary International for the convention next year. If that city had won the convention, it would have brought great things to the Danes. The restaurant tax and the Rotarian liberality, which in sparkling Denmark would naturally expand, would easily conspire, and by the time the convention had closed the Danish minister of finance could pay off the national debt. The restaurant tax is a steady source of revenue for the Danish government, but special days and conventions are very helpful. For example, on New Year's eve and morning the people in Copenhagen spent one million kroner, one-quarter of a million dollars, in restaurants and cafes. In Wivel's, said to be the finest restaurant in Europe, there were 1400 guests, and there are many similar if less expensive places in and around the capital. You can figure for yourself the state tax on this. It is enough to pay the salary of a North Carolina governor for almost an entire term, or half enough to provide a whole audit or quite enough to pay for half an audit of the finances of the State, when political controversy makes it seem wise, in an effort to exhibit the difference between cash overdraft and accrual or debit balance. This is a bit off the subject, but if Rotarians are thinking of going to Copenhagen they should be warned of that Danish restaurant tax.

McIver noted that the savage pays no tax. He rendered his service immortal by consecrating it to the interests of North Carolina, by boldly advocating and defending the rights of her youth. The Danes hold to the McIver view. Denmark finds a pillar of support in the heart of all her people. She extends maternal care to them. They love their country, whose constant solicitude is for their happiness and wholesomeness, whose ambition is to elevate them in character and intellect. What people would not love such a government? Education in that coöperative commonwealth has changed them from a poor to a prosperous people, taught them to use material prosperity to remove ignorance and prevent prejudice, shown them what power they had when they exercised it, developed a government that is bottomed upon the education and intelligence of the people. Their McIvers, if they should arise from their tombs, could not reproach the Danes with supineness and neglect of any child in Denmark. The Danes know that heavier than any tax by the government is the tax of ignorance, idleness, folly, and false pride.

CHAPTER XVIII

MARRIAGE AND DIVORCE IN DENMARK

MANY of the books say that divorce in Denmark is easy and quite popular, the statistical year book of the government adds support to this view, and proof is found also in many other places in Danish life. But when some statistics required expert interpretation, the way led to a well-known professor in the University of Copenhagen, who was described in London later by those who know as "the dean of statisticians." "How about your numerous divorces?" he was asked. He smiled and replied: "We have much divorce but not nearly so much as you."

He was speaking to a North Carolinian who until then was somewhat unfamiliar with the conditions in his own land, but had learned to respect certain features of the marriage and divorce plans in Denmark, where marriage is more or less difficult and divorce more or less easy and altogether noiseless. The statistician shortly afterwards could have twitted his visitor on the case of Vera, the Countess of Cathcart, and "moral turpitude" which made all Europe laugh, or the bill in the New York legislature which sought to keep Paris from becoming America's divorce center, but he would have been too kind to do so.

Intelligence and common sense seem to have been applied to many problems of Danish life other than those of agricultural coöperative systems, for which the Danes are perhaps best known abroad, or of the marketing of farm products, which has the respect of the world. In

Denmark this has reached such a high state of development that the owners of bad eggs are fined and an old egg has not the slightest chance to pose as a new one. The Danish divorce plan, in some important respects the most intelligent in Europe, also contains much common sense. It recognizes the wisdom and humanity of sundering the chains which bind a couple when they declare simply that they are too humane to make themselves any longer a nuisance to each other. A social crime quite as unpardonable in Denmark as that of capital punishment, which has not been inflicted there since 1892, is that of holding two people together in a loveless marriage and exposing to the view of a curious public those nauseous details which men and women so often like to feed upon.

If two parties in Denmark agree upon the necessity of dissolving their marriage they appear before an officer who, generally with the assistance of a minister, examines the case in an effort to adjust the differences and effect a reconcilation without passing judgment upon its merits. Charges of misconduct are not necessary on the part of either. "Aage," asks the reconciliation committee, "can you get along with her?" "Nay," responds Aage. "Agnete, can you get along with him?" "Nay," says she. Then they receive papers separating them for eighteen months, during which time they must stay apart and not remarry. At the end of that time absolute divorce sets in, as simply as falling off a greased log. There are no public scandals, no fighting and scratching to excite and inflame, no morbid and ugly details, so familiar in England and the United States.

"Do the parties stay apart during the year and a half?" a near divorcee whose period of patient waiting was about to expire, was asked. "Theoretically, yes," she answered. But she promptly added: "You know a wee bit of association does not really count." "And one does not become engaged again before the eighteen months are up?" "Ah, well," she answered, "perhaps a trifle, sometimes." Then she confessed that she viewed her ex-husband-to-be as a big brother who was occasionally a welcome week-end guest in her home and who frequently took for a Sunday afternoon walk their little two-year old girl. Unmarrying and remarrying are friendly and neighborly arrangements in Denmark. And if in them Denmark sins against herself and society she has the merit of doing so openly and without hypocrisy.

The Danish marriage law also seems sensible when set up against the discordant features of legislation on the subject in some of the United States where so many blunders may be seen. More than half of those states, according to the latest available information, recognize the common law or non-ceremonial marriage which requires neither license nor authorized official, a rule abolished in England a full century and a half ago. In almost half of these states persons who suffer from physical or mental diseases are not restricted from marriage. Only about one-third of them have even fair health requirements, and only eight require as a barrier against hasty marriages the advance notice of intention before a license may be issued. In a half dozen of these states girls only twelve years of age may marry, and in one of them such a child may perhaps marry without the consent of parents or guardian.

Hasty marriages which are so numerous in the United States are impossible in Denmark. For a period of two weeks the parties must publish through civil or church authorities their intention to marry. Meantime they must make many solemn declarations on honor (the equivalent of affidavits or oaths in the United States). Birth certificates must be presented. If the man is under 21 and the woman under 18 a special license may be obtained if sensible reasons are given. If the woman is under 21, she must have the consent of parents or guardian. The couple must also make declarations and give proof of sanity, but a liberal interpretation of this requirement will permit feebleminded persons to marry if they have sense enough to show the authorities that they understand what they are doing.

The couple must give proof also that they are not close blood relations, that they are not already married, and the woman, if previously married, must show that it has been more than ten months since her previous marriage was dissolved and that she is not expecting a child. The couple must also declare that they are not suffering from any sexual disease. If this declaration cannot be made by either or both then they must produce evidence from a physician that he has warned them in the presence of each other of the evil consequences of such disease, a requirement which is likely to frighten unfit persons from marriage until these dangers have been removed. Proof must be given of no illegitimate children to whom either must pay support, and that they themselves are not under regular public support.

And if there is difference in the church affiliations of the couple they must agree before the proper authorities to which church the children shall belong. Declaration must likewise be made by each of the parties that there are not in a certain section of the marriage law any obstacles to their marriage. This section makes the false confession of infidelity in a divorce case, in order to secure a quick remarriage, a barrier to remarriage for a period of two years. It is the Danish way of trying to prevent collusion, that hide-and-go-seek feature of much American divorce.

The publication of intention to marry and the details necessary in the other demands of the marriage law require a period of at least two weeks. And it is quite remarkable how many couples have the patience and endurance which such formalities exact and, with such a period to consider the new and higher relation which they seek to enter, see the test through to completion.

But with all these safeguards to marriage, there is much divorce among the Danes. Their divorce rate is one of the highest in Europe, particularly high in Copenhagen, and on the increase in the provincial cities and even in the rural communities. Among the Danes the problem of disunion is quite as insistent as that of union, though its solution seems simpler.

Under the Danish law there are two kinds of reasons for divorce. The original reasons, those present when the marriage was made, are bigamy, near blood relations, feeblemindedness (brain, sickness is the best English equivalent of the Danish word), sexual diseases, leprosy, epilepsy, impotency, misinformation in regard to the other party, compulsion, and wrong information in regard to the social identity or the past of the party such as would duly have prevented the marriage. Compulsion could not of course be very commonly offered as a reason under the conditions necessary before one can marry. Misinformation in regard to the other party would be a more or less rare reason also. The best examples of compulsion that can be found in the opinions of the courts would be cases in which one was intoxicated, or thought he was playing in a moving picture, or in which he misunderstood the language. Wrong information in regard to the social identity or the past of the party would perhaps also be an uncommon reason. A woman might represent herself as the daughter of some dignitary in Copenhagen. She might bear the name but she might be a waitress in a restaurant or a clerk in a cigar stand in a hotel lobby. Her husband could be disjoined from a union made on such misinformation. A woman, on the other hand, could be disjoined from her husband if she had been misinformed about his past,—if he had been in jail or had illegitimate children and had not fully declared the facts.

Subsequent reasons for divorce in Denmark, those appearing after the marriage, are four years' separation without papers of separation; three years' disappearance; two years' desertion (leaving without reason or the permission of the other party); infidelity; knowingly endangering the other party with sexual disease; imprisonment for more than three years for an action which in the public view is dishonorable; cruelty; bigamy; and feeblemindedness (brainsickness) which came after the marriage and continued for three years without any hope of final cure.

Relief under original or subsequent reasons may be secured from the judiciary. But this way might mean a little publicity and so the popular source of relief is the local county executive authorities. These grant divorces to parties who, having papers of separation for 18 months, agree upon the financial and other conditions of dissolution; to parties who, having such papers for 30 months, cannot agree, one of them insisting on the divorce even though the other may oppose; and to parties who show that one of the subsequent reasons for divorce is present. Separation papers may be had from the judiciary or the executives on the three grounds of lack of support, drinking or the use of other intoxicants which becomes intolerable to the other party, and such disagreement between the parties as "spoil the marriage"—the Danish equivalent of that high-minded though popular American phrase "incompatibility of temperament." This is the principal ground on which Danish marriages are dissolved, which makes the Danish plan of divorce appear noiseless and friendly.

A visitor from any one of the United States except South Carolina, where all laws permitting divorce were repealed in 1878, cannot becomingly point the finger of criticism at Denmark because of the Danish divorce rate, even though it is greatly on the increase. In 1922 there was one divorce for about every twenty marriages in Denmark and the following year there was one for every fourteen. This abnormal increase was due, however, to legislation enacted in June, 1922, which reduced the period of separation from three years to eighteen months and made certain other alterations which promptly accommodated a large waiting list. Between these two dates the increase in marriage was less than two per cent. Most of the divorces granted in these as in other years were to residents of the capital community of Copenhagen, Frederiksberg, and Gentofte, where practically one-fourth of the Danish population lives. In the United States marriages increased a little more and in North Carolina a little less than eight per cent from 1922 to 1923. But the increase in divorce during that time was eleven per cent for the United States and fourteen per cent for North Carolina. In 1923 one out of every eight marriages was dissolved by divorce in the United States and one out of every sixteen in North Carolina.

Today the United States leads the world in the number of divorces as well as in the number of grounds for divorce. The percentage increase in this means of dissolving marriage is greater than that of the increase of the population. Students of the subject estimate that, if the increase continues as it has developed during the last fifty years, by 1950 one-fourth of all marriages in the United States will be terminated by divorce and before the close of the century one-half will be thus terminated. Then, they perdict, a serious social demoralization will naturally set in quite as destructive as that which appeared in Rome during the later republic, when women calculated the year not by the consuls but by their husbands. Then family stability will be unknown, there will be much promiscuity and uncertainty regarding property and legitimacy, the encouragement of lightness and frivolity in entering marriage will increase, to be followed by much looseness and unfaithfulness afterwards, the contagion of immorality will spread, and the neglect of children who are generally the chief sufferers in the divorce movement will become greater and greater.

Already the Danes are learning that marriage involves more than personal happiness, and that it is concerned also with social responsibility. They are learning also that the clerk's certificates, wedding rings, and blessings of priests do not make marriages. It is perhaps accurate to say that they are beginning to see that every easy dissolution encourages hasty and irresponsible marriages and imperils the integrity of the home where the character of youth is formed. Hence the care with which they have framed their marriage laws. Thoughtful Danes also declare that the facility of separation and divorce is destructive of confidence, that it has been known to inflame and exaggerate trifling disputes and lead both men and women to seek often the embraces of a new wife or husband.

The Danes know that easy divorce means not only a fertile soil and seed for unhappy marriages but that it may readily become also an incentive to unfaithfulness. On the other hand they recognize divorce as a remedy which is often necessary and justifiable where danger to life or limb, or where mental or physical suffering or the rights of children demand such relief. But they deplore its use as primarily the door to experimentation in marriage and are shocked when adultery or desertion is rewarded by the right to remarry at will and perhaps make more unhappiness. Danish humanity and naturalness towards what Anglo-Saxons call irregularity probably need a higher code than is now evident. More and more are the Danes likely to see that a free and easy standard of divorce should rest upon a high and rather stringent morality.

It is the view which Americans must gain also if the dangers ahead are averted. The divorce laws of the United States, with their nearly half a hundred different grounds for this means of dissolving marriage, as bad as they are, cannot, however, be considered the cause of all the wretchedness and unhappiness of those wrecked families who exhibit themselves in divorce courts 450 or more a day throughout the year. The haphazard development of this legislation and its present confused and jumbled condition give as much trouble as could be produced by forty-eight different systems of weights and measures. It makes every day its destructive contribution to delinquency and to the instability of the family. The legal expression of this appears in the divorce statistics which also show how far the world has gone towards getting rid of permanent monogamy as the standard in modern society. But divorce statistics are not adequate measures of such instability because many marriages are dissolved by desertion, the poor man's divorce, which is as frequent as legal divorce, especially in the larger American cities. But in most of these states the need for improvement is not only in the laws for dissolving but especially in those for forming marriages, as well as in the provision of some means of education that will prepare young people safely for the tender connection.

Alarmists in Denmark and in the United States view the problem of divorce there and here as one of the most subtle menaces of the moment. They point to Rome which, after many years of soberness and abstinence from the tempting privilege, in centuries of prosperity and corruption enlarged the principle to pernicious abuse, with passion, self-interest, and caprice suggesting multitudes of motives for dissolving marriage and degrading it to a transient society of pleasure. Along with this went a great growth of vice also. And the alarmists declare that liberty of divorce does not now contribute to happiness and virtue. But one, neither an alarmist nor a sociologist, is beginning to believe that divorce whether in Denmark or the United States, whether considered as an evil or merely a sympton of evil, is primarily an attempt to solve domestic difficulties.

Such difficulties constitute constantly increasing problems which cannot be fully solved by legislation on marriage or divorce, reform in judicial procedure, and restrictions upon marriage and upon the remarriage of divorced parties. Such reforms will of course help. But systematic education of the people in social matters appears to be the safest and surest way to attack this or any other social problem. To change the habits and standards of a people chief reliance must be placed upon education. Only by and through education can right ideals of sanctioned institutions be acquired and preserved and family disorganization checked at its source. Little does the school in Denmark or elsewhere now do to inform and prepare the rising generation for the nature of family life, the adjustments and accommodations which marriage generally demands in the birth and training of children, the nature of the sex life, and similar problems of education. Not yet does the school consider these things worthy aims. Until it does, how can better conditions be reasonably expected?

The Danish statistician could have pointed his North Carolina visitor to many successful efforts of the United States to make herself appear ridiculous. He did not mention that stroke of richest irony or masterpiece of humor, the effort to exclude Vera, the Countess of Cathcart, from the pure soil of a country of contrasting absurdities, because of "moral turpitude." He did not ask whether the bill introduced in the New York legislature to make invalid for a New Yorker any divorce obtained in Paris was an effort to protect a great native industry against foreign competition. He was not so churlish. He did not even inquire why a Gutenberg Bible brought in the United States a price of more than one hundred thousand dollars.

But the European press was not so kind. Editorials and cartoons of quite caustic character were abundant. And the French Ministry of Justice in statistical statements vigorously denied the statements of the New York legislator that Paris courts are divorce mills for disgruntled American couples. This department of the French government reported that only 120 divorces were granted last year to American applicants. These were of course granted chiefly to wealthy Americans; but it was maintained that this was a remarkably low figure in view of the facts that there were nearly 150,000 American tourists in France in 1925 and that the American colony in Paris numbers nearly 50,000. Paris officials noted at the same time that while the Paris courts were granting 120 decrees, the courts in New York dispensed similar renewals of single blessedness in 4500 cases.

CHAPTER XIX

The Decay of Romance

SOME TIME ago a rather well known English novelist, some of whose writings are noted for their convincing love passages, said that the present generation did not know how to fall in love. Previously he had got into severe trouble by stating on a public platform that all women were jungle cats and that if men were wise they would put the women back behind those domestic bars, which in reality, he thought, made the only safe cage for their savage felinity. Subsequently, when the women protested, he explained that this statement should not be taken seriously, but his apology availed him nothing. The women persisted in regarding him as a hater of their sex.

A railway journey of a little less than two hours from the Danish capital brings you to the town of Elsinore which probably has lost but little if any of its picturesqueness since the days when the majesty of Denmark marched before the battlements of Castle Kronborg, which was made, you may recall, the scene of a famous Shakesperean tragedy. It was here that Hamlet heard at midnight the ominous spectre cry, and it is here that one may even now indulge the imagination and try to conjure up the extravagant and erring spirits of Horatio and Marcellus.

The grim old castle with its apparently impenetrable casements, its copper-sheathed towers and its prickly spires which rise high and proudly towards the heavens, frowns over the gleaming waters of Elsinore Sound which it was built in the sixteenth century to guard. From this castle for nearly three hundred years Danish kings claimed and levied burdensome duties on the Baltic shipping. Even today it seems to regard grimly the Swedish coast over which it has so long watched. Its massive walls appear in an almost perfect state of preservation, and the edges of the carvings are still sharp. Deep into the dungeons in the bowels of the earth below it you may descend to places which, your fancy may tell you, are inhabited by bats and dragons. In the deepest and darkest of these sat (perhaps still sits), according to tradition, old Holger Danske, a Danish national hero of Scandinavian origin. He is clad in steel and iron. His long beard hangs down over a marble table into which it has grown. Holger Danske sleeps and dreams, and in his dreams he sees all that goes on in Denmark. Every Christmas, says the legend, an angel comes and tells him that what he has dreamed is true, that Denmark is in no danger, and that he may go to sleep again in peace. But if real peril should ever threaten his beloved country then Holger Danske will arouse himself so vigorously that the table of stone will be shivered to pieces as he draws out his beard. Then he will come forth and strike with all his might and all the world will resound with the combat in defense of his land.

Every Dane knows and delights to relate or refer to the story of Holger Danske. The tradition persists through Danish patriotism though in reality only two fragments of stone remain in the dungeon, one a part of Holger's table and the other his pillow. Near by also there are two other supreme deceptions, but these the ignorance and credulity of American and English tourists have helped to make possible. So when you go to Elsinore you should ask about Hamlet's grave and the spring of Ophelia, if you would be regarded as a regular tourist. If it is autumn or winter you may find the grave somewhat run down because it is not built up until spring, just before the tourists begin to come. Hamlet is of course not buried in or near Elsinore. And if you are agreeable to an obliging English-speaking Dane you may learn about the hoax without having to pay a guide.

In the good old days when the Danish kings were yet collecting sound duties at that point, myriads of ships stopped at Elsinore to pay them and to be plundered, perhaps, by the inhabitants. Each fresh English sailor on his first visit, like most American tourists now, asked to be shown the grave of Hamlet. On the outside of the village, in the garden of a resident merchant, stood one of thousands of barrows which were scattered so plentifully over Denmark. This was somehow or other settled upon as a very popular last resting place for the remains of Shakespeare's famous character. Many visitors greatly harassed and tormented this merchant as they came to view the spot. At his own expense, so the story goes, he made a mound at another point near by, on which he placed a cross and a badly blurred inscription which fixed the date of Hamlet's death on the 32d of October, old style, in a year not given. The joke worked well, satisfied the curious visitors, and permitted the merchant to go about his work undisturbed. But such a digression may not be pardonable, because Hamlet and Ophelia have nothing whatever to do with the subject of this note.

It concerns rather the contrast between what must have been the romantic and spectacular if often brutal methods of Viking love-making and the rather matter-of-fact methods which the Danes seem now to employ. The Danish maiden may be romantic but she appears very realistic and matter-of-fact. Seldom is she now courted at home and in chaperonage as formerly, but in park and restaurant and club, often in the smartest and most fashionable clothes and the most modern hair cuts which range all the way from a simple bob to the Eton crop. She would doubtless laugh heartily at the Danish equivalent of "Drink to me only with thine eyes," or some other favorite love song which the Vikings accompanied with the club and in older days moved her mother and grandmother. "Wine!" she should probably exclaim. "Surely not wine, the plebeian, vulgar stuff. Order up cocktails, a beautiful dinner, and then liqueurs." Her matter-of-fact suitor would never be seen to put his hand to his heart or kneel before her in amorous protestation, or grab her by hair or hands to make her do his bidding. If he should do so, such capers would seem gleeful if not quite ridiculous to her. No longer does she waste a blush under her rouge or languish or fade away as was the fashion years ago. She has changed. Her change has helped to change him. Now he has time and courage only to say: "Now, look here, Agnete, you know that I am really quite fond of you," rarely ever reaching the fatal word "love."

Perhaps conditions have changed elsewhere as well. The new conditions represent the revolt against the old attitude of men towards women and of women towards men. The revolt against chivalry is obvious in Denmark. Here women have left the pedestal where so long they were kept, looked up to, given vain and empty compliments, considered as somewhat refined clay, the guardians, if feeble ones, of the morality and purity of the world about them, and sheltered against the wickedness and freedom in the world of masculinity. As a reward for this glory and shelter the Danish woman was formerly held, like women elsewhere, in almost complete servitude and subjection to the men who furnish her with opinions, owned her soul and body, and generally her property, if she had any. She was denied all but a few activities, was not permitted to compete with men, but was compelled to confine her interests and tasks to those which men could not or would not do, such as having children, washing dishes, scrubbing floors, and the like. That day is gone in Denmark.

Even in these conditions, however, it is said that home life in Denmark has wide fascination and charm. The domestic traditions were strong and strongly adhered to in practically all classes. Some of that strength yet remains, despite many startling modern changes. In the better class homes the women still rule and their rule is marked generally by gentleness. Almost all Danish women are gentle in speech and manner. Excellent physical education from early years and life in the open give them grace and charm. Generally the Danish woman is an excellent cook, having learned the art from her own mother or older sisters or in the excellent domestic science departments of the schools. In other ways also she is equipped and trained to give to the household over which she presides an attractive intimacy and cosiness.

But even in Denmark woman has discovered that she was probably not on a pedestal at all, that she was not actually worshiped, that it was all the fraudulent excuse of a man to keep her from a freedom which she craved. In time she won it, after some struggles which were now and then marked as in other parts of the world by a bit of violence, sometimes of quite scandalous nature. Her enfranchisement was to prove, however, only a vestibule to a larger and more varied freedom which she soon came to demand and in large part has gained. In this, she believes, the behests of love are fulfilled. Old ideals have begun to give way to new ones, new economic conditions have thrown her into the society, the activities, and the occupations of men, and promise to make her much more nearly the equal of man than ever before. One result is a certain practical realism now seen generally in Denmark and which must have been unknown in the days when wooing required the club of the cave man or a gentler method such as the holding of hands at concerts, dances, quilting and serenade parties, and the reading together of poetry in which love and dove, mine and thine, and die and sigh could be made to rhyme.

The new freedom of the Danish woman has had much to do with producing this condition. Today she has perhaps the highest sex status in all Europe. In Denmark little of sex difference remains. Practically all Danish women have their own work of one kind or another. They are dentists and doctors, lawyers and merchants, and architects, and members of parliament and of the cabinet, as well as telephone and telegraph operators, hotel waitresses, typists, secretaries, office assistants, and the like. Every morning and afternoon the streets of Copenhagen and of the provincial towns and cities are filled with their bicycles taking them to and from work. Through her work the Danish woman has won for herself a somewhat unique place in the economic world.

Moreover, she has won what appears to be a sensible marriage status. She is the equal of her "man," the word which she uses for husband. She is not his tool or chattel or butterfly or clothes horse, or his light o'love, licensed or otherwise. She is his wife and a human being at the same time, good natured, democratic, his associate and partner. She has set out with him confidently on that sometimes rocky road of matrimony to solve its ever persistent problem of merging and coalescing lovers into comrades and friends. To the average Danish woman marriage does not appear to be a respectabilized side or back door through which she hopes to escape work or the scorn and discomfiture of spinsterhood. It is an important life enterprise with her. She is likely to enter it as a solemn engagement to be maintained until death or the judge dissolves it. But if it is a failure or threatens to be she does not have to wait for the grim reaper. She finds in the Danish divorce law a less painful way and this she does not hesitate to take.

The Danish woman is the most natural and human to be found anywhere. She calls things by their right names. A spade is a spade and not a useful implement used in agriculture. Subjects which among English and Americans are so often made to seem ugly and of doubtful propriety are discussed freely and openly and with great dignity and ease by Danish men and women.

Their conversation is remarkably free from coarseness and suggestion, but there is nothing prudish about them. They do not teach their children that they were found in beechtrees or bulrushes. The women have even been known to tell their own ages, sometimes perhaps with dangerous accuracy. The birthdays of Danish women are not movable feasts. Nor do men need to perjure themselves to be agreeable to Danish women.

There is humanity also in the public attitude towards the sins of the flesh which in Denmark are regarded as joint responsibilities. The woman who has loved not wisely but too well in the primrose path of dalliance is not turned out of doors and made to do penance in white sheet and candle. She is not the object of scorn as she so often is in some other parts of the world. She is regarded with sympathy; and humane provision is made for her and her child just as if the union of which he is the fruit had been blessed by holy priest or vulgar squire. There are no tear-stained, white-faced Magdalenes in Denmark.

This may be a healthy condition. In time it may lead to refinement and subtlety in love making and mating. It may give love a proper chance. But is there danger that by the new condition of freedom which surrounds the Danish woman she may of necessity come to be considered more and more like man? Already she has copied his clothes and his hair cut and many of his bad habits and his foibles. Equality is the shibboleth of the modern Danish woman. Equality she craves. Perhaps she needs to learn that differences between men and women are not necessarily defects, but are rather decrees of nature; and nature is not to be set aside, altered, or made bankrupt by suffrage legislation or by other conditions which bring new emancipations to women. What is to be gained, the Danes are asked, by merging their men and women into colorless identity, by forcing stupid equality? No favor is conferred on two mountains by filling up the valley between them.

No longer does the Danish woman, for dear life's sake, have to choose a good provider of material things as a husband (perhaps quite incidentally the father of her children). Nor is the Dane considered foolish because he falls in love with a woman who is not known for her skill as cook or housemaid, but has rather an adorable chin, a heavenly laugh, or movements that suggest music, —something which the mysterious "life force" has struggled to develop and produce from the primeval slime and now struggles to preserve and improve. She has practically all the rights formerly monopolized by men, who have, however, apparently not yet discovered that she surrenders slowly and quite grudgingly those unique privileges she has always enjoyed, such as pretending to sit on a pedestal, demanding and seeming to relish and believe packs of pious lies men tell her about her good looks, her form, her cleverness, her capacity for managing large affairs, the daintiness of her ankles, and the like. She must laugh also at the stupidity of the men who continue to buy her theatre tickets, pay the taxi fare and the dinner check, without respecting her new freedom and rights and insisting that the rules of a Dutch treat apply.

Perhaps in this changed status of Danish women appears the hall mark of civilization, an advance rather than a retrogression. Perhaps not.

The Decay of Romance 221

Civilization is in large part a matter of taste and outlook. The merits of the case are not here argued. It is stated as it has impressed one visitor in Denmark.

The growth in immorality and vice in the urban communities of Denmark some people charge to the new freedom of women and to the increase in divorce. Many Danes seem to hold this view. Copenhagen seems to compare not unfavorably, however, with London or Paris or other European capitals in the problems of immorality. Until 1906 prostitution was controlled in Copenhagen by means of license and medical inspection, but since that date there has been no control and prostitution is no longer legally recognized. Yet the moral life of Copenhagen is apparently quite unwholesome. Women are not permitted to earn a living solely by means of prostitution, however, and must show the police if challenged that they have other means of subsistence. The abolition of professional prostitution seems to have led to a large increase in the number of girls and young women who traffic in this tragic business, many of them apparently for pleasure. Many night clubs in Copenhagen are more or less shameless places of rendezvous for the immoral.

The commercial attaché of one of the foreign governments in one of his annual reports noted the acute housing problem in Copenhagen which he thought was due in part to the large number of unmarried women who maintained their own flats or rooms instead of living with their families. This condition has been cited by some as evidence not only of the increased freedom the Danish women are demanding for themselves but also of the ease with which immorality is practiced in the capital. Moreover, Denmark is notorious for the large number of children who are born out of wedlock. For the country at large one out of every nine children is illegitimate and in Copenhagen the figure is practically one out of four. The new status of women and the large freedom that is usually permitted young people during engagements may help to explain this condition. Engagements are often long and not infrequently broken, though they are practically always rather formally made.

In certain rural sections of Denmark, however, where until recently two marriage ceremonies were required, the explanation of illegitimacy is in part historical. Between the preliminary and the final ceremony, which was often postponed for economic or other reasons, many children were born, but no disgrace attached to parents or children because the latter were born out of wedlock. There has been a marked change in the public attitude toward such children. The old attitude was hostile. Today it is very humane.

Here perhaps as in other parts of the world great changes are taking place. There is violence in the conflict between the old order which seems to be passing and the new which seeks to make its own way and place. So often does one hear it said in Denmark: "Before the war it was thus and so. Now it is so different." Perhaps it should be so. New generations strike out into untried paths. In Denmark the older people as in the United States seem to cling to much of their fathers' faith and to have built upon and to have found rest in that philosophy of life. Little of such basis is discernible, however, in the views of most of the young people in Denmark who reveal disturbing evidences of unrest, of aspiration, and of doubt. Perhaps the one group is saddened by the memory of the old which is passing and the other is impatient with the unfulfilled promise of the new which has not yet fully arrived.

The well known English novelist may or may not be right. The youth of today may or may not know how to fall in or make love. Women may or may not be jungle cats. The questions are not argued. But a visitor to Denmark, reviewing her virile past and observing certain conditions in her life today, naturally wonders how much longer Holger Danske will be permitted to sleep until the devil rather than an angel shall awaken him. Then Kronborg Castle will collapse and the disturbance will resound throughout the world.

CHAPTER XX

SOCIAL WELFARE

I HAVE read your articles on Denmark and against your native State," rebuked a life-long friend a few days ago. "Why don't you find out what we are doing in North Carolina? Read the current number of the *National Geographic Magazine* and the New York *Sun* for last Saturday, which praised the Tar Heels, and point with pride to conditions in your own home State." It was a few days before the democratic state convention, which every two years sets the pride-pointing styles in North Carolina. This devotee of democracy was polishing his nails for that pride pointing party which dodged the proposal for a respectable school term and got bow-legged by straddling the Australian ballot issue.

The Danes, if yet another contrast between the two communities be permitted, appear a trifle more courageous in facing real social and political problems. Good schools have purified their politics, dignified their ways of government, and so enlightened the people generally that hocus pocus of whatever variety has less chance as a guide of life in Denmark than *The Origin of Species* would have as a prayer book in Tennessee.

Big issues are faced squarely in Denmark. The Danish code of social legislation is broad in its humanity and unexcelled in practicability, and there as elsewhere is discernible a very close relation between economic and social conditions and the development of such legislation. Seventy-five years ago an industrial development began among the Danes and created a working population under looser and more uncertain economic influences than before. The need for social legislative measures at once arose. Trade unions began to gain some strength during the last quarter of the last century but for some time these were of minor influence and apart from a few acts for the protection of workmen their effect was limited in scope. It was not until the last decade of that century that social legislation began in earnest. Since then more and more questions have been taken up, there was marked progress in social reforms during the years immediately following the war, and today Denmark is in company with and in some respects quite ahead of most countries in advanced social legislation and control. Even the Danish industries, whose products increasingly find their way to the markets of the world, rest upon a sensible social basis.

Such a highly developed code of social legislation in an agricultural country may appear out of harmony with the experiences of other countries and communities, including the United States. The fact should not seem so strange, however, when it is recalled that Denmark is a commonwealth of small and medium sized farms, and that social legislation there on many points covers these independent farmers as well as the so-called industrial classes. It should also be kept in mind that during the last generation a rather comprehensive industry has developed in Denmark affecting many people in addition to those engaged in commerce, transportation, and shipping. Today about four-ninths of the Danish people live in the country and one-third of them engage in agriculture. Perhaps two-ninths live in Copenhagen, the most important commercial city of the Baltic and the northern countries, a similar number live in eighty-odd provincial towns, for the most part of quite ancient origin, and the remainder live in small villages and suburbs.

For many generations Denmark has had certain forms of public aid, many voluntary societies for mutual support and private charities. It was not until quite recent years, however, that an insistent demand arose for real social legislation. Industrial changes, the introduction of machinery, improved means of transportation, and other conditions, necessitated the interference of society in behalf of the working classes. The rise of the rural underclass to a position of leadership, the labor movement, and ideas from abroad led to reform. There was much discussion among the people themselves, by legislative committees, in the press, and elsewhere. Constitutional obstacles were encountered, however, and there were occasional constitutional struggles. Finally all such difficulties were removed, the middle and upper classes became sympathetic towards the underprivileged, and in time all turned to the common task of improving the conditions of Danish workers of all kind and condition.

The Danes are a pioneer people in courageous experiments for the social betterment of workers. The working people in the urban communities disclose the same aptitude for team work and collective action as the farmers display by uniting in coöperative societies. The principle is that of protection through self-help. The people themselves have provided many forms of protection through voluntary insurance against illness, accident, unemployment, and the like, and there are public pensions for widows, for children, and for the aged, and other forms of public aid which the unfortunate may accept without losing civic rights, such, for example, as the right of suffrage. The workmen through trade unions took and still take the initiative and they are assisted in their reforms by the government. The work of social welfare has been promoted, therefore, by agencies growing out of working men's organizations. Legislation in Denmark quickly follows the demonstration of the need for it. When the advantage of a proposed measure is shown the people, its enactment into law seems a natural and easy sequence. The high level of education and intelligence among the masses of the people is the explanation of this fact.

Sickness benefit societies began in Denmark before there was sickness benefit legislation, but they have reached their present high and beneficial condition by means of state aid and state control. Insurance is voluntary in such organizations, which are self-governing, but by giving aid the state is enabled to gain some control which is generally exercised principally by giving advice and guidance. Membership is open to all ordinary workers and to men and women of the same economic status, such as small farmers, artisans, tradespeople, civil service employees, and the like. In order to receive state aid, the rules of a sick benefit club must be approved and it must submit to state supervision. As a rule it must have as many as two hundred members. Last year there were sixteen hundred approved organizations of this kind in Denmark, with a membership of about one and a half millions,—nearly half the entire Danish population.

Most of the clubs are comparatively small, but in the towns and especially in Copenhagen, many have large memberships. The insurance in all essentials also covers the members' children and adopted children below fifteen years of age. In case of illness, members received free medical assistance, hospital treatment, maternity benefits, and sick pay for at least twenty-six weeks a year. Medical aid comprises about one-half of the expenditure. The subscriptions of the members produce about two-thirds of the funds necessary for this service. The subsidy from the state amounts to about one-third, approximately seventy-five cents a member, plus one-fourth of the outlays towards compulsory grants. There is a further public subsidy, one-half from the state and one-half from the municipality, for special expenses of members suffering from chronic illness.

Municipalities may also assist clubs to give members hospital treatment for half of the already very low hospital charges. Denmark has a highly developed hospital service supported almost exclusively by the municipalities or the counties. These institutions provide free treatment and assistance to the poor, and in the case of epidemic and venereal diseases treatment is free for all. Last year the central government expended thirteen million kroner (about three and a quarter million dollars) for this purpose, in addition to nearly one million dollars to combat tuberculosis and a half million dollars to control epidemics. The local Danish governments spent for public health and medical purposes more than eight million dollars.

Denmark spends much less in alms for the poor than in pensions for the aged. As early as 1891 and before any other country Denmark introduced old age pensions for the deserving poor above sixty years of age. The plan, while free of contribution by those receiving pensions, was quite unconnected with the administration of poor relief, application for which has generally been a last resort, because those who receive such relief lose the right to vote and other privileges of citizenship. The early plan was administered by the municipal or local government officers who decided each case upon its merits. It failed to stimulate industry and thrift, however, and the plan was revised and strengthened. Today the pensioner must comply with certain conditions of age and respectability. The amount of the pension depends upon locality, sex and matrimonial status. One may receive the pension at the age of sixty-five, but for each year that he postpones the enjoyment of the annuity between sixty-five and sixty-eight the pensioner gets ten per cent more.

The yearly pension for a married couple in Copenhagen, for example, who do not begin to receive the annuity until one of them is sixty-eight years old and the other at least sixty-five, amounts to 1440 kroner (about $380). The lowest pension, that is, one that is granted to a single woman of sixty-five living in a rural community where living expenses would not be so great as in the city, is 372 kroner (about $93.00). These fixed amounts are granted in full, however, only when the income of the person does not exceed half the fixed amount of the pension plus 100 kroner (about $25). In the case of larger incomes larger deductions are made. In addition to the pension the person may receive medical aid and be received also in one of the many homes for the aged. These homes are in striking contrast to the "poor houses" still found in so many American states. They are attractive and well appointed and provide adequately for the last days of the old people, who are treated with respect and tenderness and die without the stigma of poverty but with the benediction of public esteem. Last year pensions were paid by the municipalities to more than one hundred thousand people in amounts which total 72 million kroner (about 18 million dollars), seven-twelfths of which the central government refunded.

Nowhere perhaps is the welfare of workers better protected than among the Danish people. Besides the insurance and public relief plans, which constitute one of the most important parts of social legislation, there is comprehensive control of hours and conditions of labor. The first act for the protection of workmen was passed in 1873 and restricted the work of children and juveniles in factories and workshops. A few years later additional legislation was enacted to protect workers against machinery in factories. Under the present factory act authority is given the inspectors to demand good and safe hygienic and sanitary conditions in all working places. Children under fourteen years of age are prohibited from working in industry, handicrafts, or transportation, or in any branches of such undertakings; and young persons between the ages of fourteen and eighteen cannot be employed in such undertakings at night.

Denmark has been called a paradise for children. Adequate educational opportunity is provided for them all, in good schools of long terms and with excellently trained teachers. Sensible compulsory school attendance and child labor laws constantly work together in the interests of child life instead of landlords and mill owners. Whether legitimate or illegitimate, Danish children are fully safeguarded by law and a close and rigid system of labor and factory inspection. Moreover, for four weeks after childbirth women must not work in factories unless they hold certificates from the medical inspectors to the effect that such work does not endanger the health of the mother or child. And these certificates are difficult to secure. During the period when such a mother is not allowed to work she may receive public aid, and the civic disabilities of the ordinary poor relief do not attach to her.

The mother of an illegitimate child is also entitled to public aid which, in case the father does not pay the contribution for which he is liable, is paid in advance by the municipality or county, if such a mother is in need, and if she does not have other illegitimate children. Such aid is not regarded as poor relief to her but to the child's father, who is deprived of certain civic rights, such as the right of suffrage, if he does not refund the amount. Aid is also granted, half by the state and half by the town or county, to orphans and widows' children below fourteen years of age, in cases of need. Eight thousand widows with about eighteen thousand children were aided in this manner last year at an expense of about two and a half million kroner (quite above a half million dollars).

In addition to all these public measures, private philanthropy, which often takes the form of many small anonymous gifts, is actively interested in child life. Thousands of free meals are every year served to school children during recesses. Useful fresh air societies are also numerous. In the summer, generally in July, several thousands of the city and town school children are given free transportation to farms and back again in time for the opening of school. Hospitable farmers receive these children who do light farm chores and spend much time in wholesome forms of recreation, swimming, fishing, and playing. The "children's trains" filled with multitudes of happy youth are said to be lively sights as they move joyously to the countryside. There is also the children's "help day," a new holiday which love for childhood has added to the calendar of Denmark. The custom is best known in Copenhagen. On a specified day once a year hundreds of voluntary solicitors may be heard and seen in the streets rattling tiny tin boxes which receive from the passers-by small coins for the aid of children. Booths may be seen in squares and in busy corners in the streets which often become so congested that traffic stops. There are sideshows and other attractions to induce the people to contribute to the cause, and there are processions and pageants representing childhood. This custom is another spontaneous expression of coöperative life, and although it is not always lacking in emotional color, it gives further evidence of the Danish belief that a commonwealth can move forward only upon the feet of her children.

The workmen's compensation legislation dealing with accidental injuries contracted while working is another evidence of interest in public welfare. The money is provided by insurance premiums paid by the employers, and the legislation covers not only the workers in all trades but any one doing work for another. Moreover, small employers and intelligent workers may voluntarily insure themselves and their wives. One of the most remarkable features of the Danish compensation legislation is the benefit for permanent invalidity or death. The insurance is effected in competing private companies which are supervised by a national insurance board, and the settlement of the question of liability for compensation is made by government officials. Denmark has also developed successfully unemployment insurance which is based upon contributions by the members who are thus stimulated to saving reserve funds. The contributions of the members cover about three-fifths of the cost of unemployment insurance, and the State contributes about one-fifth and the local communities about one-fifth. The funds are subject to government supervision and are managed in conjunction with the trades unions, an arrangement which makes for lower costs of administration. Closely connected with this form of insurance is the public labor exchange or employment bureau, the operating expenses of which are borne by the centra government and the municipalities or counties. The last expedient open to anyone who cannot by organization provide for himself or family is the ordinary poor relief, with the unpleasant consequences which result from it: the loss of the vote, and the unfavorable reputation which public opinion attaches to one accepting poor relief. Modern social legislation, however, covers the great bulk of cases so that only about one per cent of the total Danish population receives public poor relief.

The attitude of the government is quite liberal in dealing with the problems of unemployment, public subsidies for such purposes amounting to about forty per cent of the income of unemployment funds. These subsidies consist of grants by the central government and by municipalities or counties. Last year the subsidy of the central government was eight million kroner (about two million dollars) and the subsidies from the local government amounted to about three million kroner. Under the ordinary pre-war conditions and during the first years of the war the unemployment associations were able to meet their obligations on the insurance basis, but unemployment greatly increased between 1917 and 1921 and the government was compelled to grant increased sums toward the solution of the problem. In 1922 a special unemployment fund was established for use in the event of extraordinary unemployment, by granting relief to unemployed people, and providing courses of training for them. At that time the central government granted the sum of seven million kroner and by the end of the year 1922-23 an additional sum of ten million kroner. In the ordinary course of events the Danish unemployment fund receives a government grant equivalent to 10 per cent of the total contribution of the ordinary members plus one-third of the total amount disbursed by them. The employers pay five kroner per year for every man employed by them, and the local governments pay one-third of the amount expended in extraordinary unemployment relief. The inspection of unemployment funds is made by a special government board working in conjunction with various committees in which both employers and workers are represented.

For the purpose of maintaining hygienic and housing standards in Denmark there is a national board of health and numerous medical officers, each of whom has the direction of a district and exercises ordinary hygienic supervision. In addition there are many local boards of health, found in every town and in most of the rural communities. The public hospital service is also highly developed in Denmark. Altogether there are 14,000 beds in the ordinary public hospitals and there are also special sanatoria with accommodations for about 2,000 patients. Institutions for the accommodation of lunatics and mentally deficient people have accommodations for 5,000 patients.

The conditions of the Danish working classes have improved considerably since these advanced social measures have been effective. Working hours in industry have decreased from eleven in 1872 to eight at the present time. Wages have greatly increased. As a result of social and sanitary legislation mortality has greatly decreased during the last generation. The mortality rate is today reported lower than that of any other country. Particular progress has been made in reducing infant mortality and tuberculosis. Statistics also show a great decrease in the use of intoxicating liquors and the number of suicides among the Danes.

From the sensible plan of Danish social legislation most American states may learn many lessons. In those states too many of the people living on farms and by means of farming are denied adequate protection and an equitable share in the prosperity that is enjoyed by most of those people who are engaged in industrial development. In most of those states, particularly in the South Atlantic region, too many people are yet unable to read and write. Too many of the school children are retarded by short term schools and poor teachers. It has been known for some time that most of those retarded children are in the rural communities which are so inadequately developed. Too many babies die in the United States every year, most of them before they are a year old, as a result of the parents' ignorance of the simplest laws of child welfare. Too many of the farm workers in the United States are in the toils of the vicious system of tenancy, owning not an inch of the soil they live on nor a single shingle in the roofs under which they sleep. The Danes have been able through education and coöperation to reduce social injustice and to increase the well-being of all the people.

www.ingramcontent.com/pod-product-compliance
Lightning Source LLC
Chambersburg PA
CBHW021359290426
44108CB00010B/307